KU-441-223

Stories of Detection and Mystery

Level 5

Selected and retold by E. J. H. Morris and D. J. Mortimer
Series Editors: Andy Hopkins and Jocelyn Potter

Pearson Education Limited
Edinburgh Gate, Harlow,
Essex CM20 2JE, England
and Associated Companies throughout the world.

ISBN 0 582 419395

First published in the Longman Simplified English Series 1965
First published in the Longman Fiction Series 1993
This adaptation first published in 1997
Second impression 1997
This edition first published 1999

NEW EDITION
5 7 9 10 8 6 4

We are grateful to the following for permission to reproduce simplified versions of
copyright material: authors' agents on behalf of The Royal Literary Fund for 'The Blue
Cross' and 'The Invisible Man' by G. K. Chesterton from *The Innocence of Father Brown*;
authors' agents/The Putnam Publishing Group for 'Philomel Cottage' by Agatha Christie
from *The Listerdale Mystery* (UK title) copyright © Agatha Christie Mallowan 1934 and
Witness for the Prosecution and Other Stories (US title) copyright © Agatha Christie Mallowan
1924; authors' agents on behalf of Charles Gordon Clark for 'The Heel' (simplified title
'An Unpleasant Man') by Cyril Hare from *The Best Detective Stories of Cyril Hare*, published
Faber & Faber Ltd.; W. Foulsham & Co. Ltd. for 'The Hoodoo Theatre' (simplified title
'The Unlucky Theatre') by Elliot O'Donnell; N. J. R. James for 'The Mezzotint' by M. R.
James from *Collected Ghost Stories*, published by Edward Arnold Ltd.; authors' agents on
behalf of P. & M. Youngman Carter Ltd. for 'Family Affair' by Margery Allingham; Eidos plc
for 'The Case of the Thing That Whimpered' by Dennis Wheatley from *Gunmen, Gallants
& Ghosts*.

This edition copyright © Penguin Books Ltd 1999
Cover design by Bender Richardson White

Set in 11/14pt Bembo
Printed in Spain by Mateu Cromo, S.A. Pinto (Madrid)

*All rights reserved; no part of this publication may be reproduced, stored
in a retrieval system, or transmitted in any form or by any means,
electronic, mechanical, photocopying, recording or otherwise, without the
prior written permission of the Publishers.*

Published by Pearson Education Limited in association with
Penguin Books Ltd, both companies being subsidiaries of Pearson Plc

For a complete list of titles available in the Penguin Readers series please write to your local
Pearson Education office or contact: Penguin Readers Marketing Department,
Pearson Education, Edinburgh Gate, Harlow, Essex, CM20 2JE.

Contents

Introduction

This collection includes offerings from some of the most famous British writers of detective and mystery stories of the first half of the twentieth century. Although the stories are quite different from each other, each has an everyday setting in which unexpected and often strange events begin to take place. By the end of the story, the mystery is solved. Sometimes there is a common-sense explanation; sometimes there is a suggestion of dark forces at work. A number of the central characters in the stories are detectives who have become very well known over the years.

Gilbert Keith Chesterton (1874–1936) was an English writer who produced thousands of poems and stories on a wide variety of subjects. Chesterton's best-known works are his mystery and detective stories. Some of his characters are unforgettable, particularly the priest Father Brown. Although he appears to be rather ordinary and even a little stupid, Father Brown solves the most difficult mysteries in his slow, careful and extremely polite way. Forty-eight Father Brown stories appeared between 1911 and 1935; two are included in this collection.

Agatha Christie (1890–1976) is one of the most famous detective writers ever. She wrote over eighty books and is the most widely translated writer in the English language. Many of her books feature detectives. Of these, perhaps the best known are Hercule Poirot and Miss Marple. 'Philomel Cottage' is unusual in that it does not feature a detective or a group of suspects, but tells the story from the point of view of the person who, we come to discover, is under threat of death.

Cyril Hare (1900–58) is the pen name of Alfred Alexander Gordon Clark. He was a lawyer and judge as well as a mystery writer, and his writing comes directly from his knowledge of criminals and the law. Cyril Hare wrote nine books and some fine short stories. In 'An Unpleasant Man' it is the policeman who notices something that seems unimportant, but is found to be central to the solution of the mystery.

Elliott O'Donnell (1872–1965) had a lifelong interest in ghosts and mysterious or unexplained events, and produced several serious books on the subject, such as *Some Haunted Houses of England and Wales* (1908) and *Strange Sea Mysteries* (1926). He also carried this interest into his stories, a good example of which is 'The Unlucky Theatre', included in this collection. His best-known book is *The Sorcery Club* (1912), about three men who put the dark secrets of Atlantis to their own evil use.

The setting for 'The Mezzotint' is very ordinary. But into this Montague Rhodes James (1862–1936) suddenly introduces unexplained and frightening events. James wrote four collections of ghost stories. In his working life he was a highly respected historian who produced many books on his subject.

Margery Allingham (1904–66) was a social historian as well as a writer of mystery stories. Her most famous character is the detective Albert Campion, who appears in many of her books as well as in this short story, 'Family Affair'. Like Chesterton's Father Brown, Campion is a character who surprises those who do not take him seriously.

Dennis Wheatley (1897–1977) wrote many types of books, including mystery and crime stories, and has been widely translated. His best-known characters are the secret agents Roger Brook and Gregory Sallust. 'The Case of the Thing That Whimpered' appears at first to be a ghost story, but the mysterious noises belong to a more familiar world.

The Blue Cross   *G. K. Chesterton*

Early one morning the boat arrived at Harwich and from it poured a crowd of travellers. Among them the man that we must follow did not look out of place in any way – nor did he wish to. There was nothing out of the ordinary about him, except a slight difference between the relaxed look of his holiday clothes and the rather serious expression on his face. He was wearing a pale grey coat, a white shirt, and a silver hat. His thin face was dark in comparison and ended in a short black beard that looked rather Spanish. He was smoking. No one would have thought that the grey coat hid a loaded gun, that the pocket of his white shirt held a police card, or that the hat covered one of the most powerful brains in Europe. For this was Valentin himself, the head of the Paris police and the most famous detective in the world; and he was coming from Brussels to London to make the greatest arrest of the century.

Flambeau was in England. The police of three countries had tracked the great criminal at last from Ghent to Brussels, from Brussels to the Hook of Holland; and it was thought that he would make use of the unfamiliarity and confusion of the international meeting of priests which was then taking place in London. Probably he would travel as some unimportant clerk or secretary connected with it; but, of course, Valentin could not be certain. Nobody could be certain about Flambeau.

It is many years now since this great criminal, Flambeau, suddenly stopped causing trouble; and when he stopped there was relief around the world. In his best days (I mean, of course, his worst) Flambeau was an internationally known figure. Almost every morning the daily papers announced that he had escaped punishment for one unbelievable crime by breaking the law a second time. He was a Frenchman of great strength, size and daring, and the wildest stories were told of the amusing uses that he made of his physical abilities: how he turned a judge upside down and stood him on his head, 'to clear his mind'; how he ran down the street with a policeman under each arm. But it must be said of him that his unusual physical strength was generally employed in bloodless ways; his crimes were chiefly those of clever robberies. It was he who ran the great Tyrolean Milk Company in London, with no cows, no delivery vehicles, and no milk, but with more than a thousand customers. He did this by the simple operation of moving the little milk cans outside people's doors to the doors of his own customers. Many of his crimes were extremely simple. It is said that he once repainted all the house numbers in a street in the middle of the night just to lead one traveller into a trap. It is quite certain that he invented a public letterbox which could be moved from place to place. This he put up in quiet corners of the town in the hope that a stranger might drop a cheque or bank note into it. Lastly, he was known to be very quick and active; in spite of his large size, he could jump as well as any insect and hide in the treetops like a monkey. For this reason the great Valentin, when he set out to find Flambeau, knew very well that his adventures would not end when he had found him.

But how would he find him? The great Valentin still did not have a plan.

There was one thing about himself which Flambeau could not change, whatever he did to his appearance, and that was his unusual height. If Valentin's quick eye had seen a tall apple seller, a tall soldier, or even a fairly tall woman, he might have arrested them immediately. But just as a lion cannot pretend to be a mouse, so there was nobody now on his train who could be Flambeau dressed as someone else. Valentin had already made certain that he was not among the people on the boat; and only six other people had got on the train at Harwich or during the journey. There was a short railway official travelling up to London, three fairly short farmers picked up two stations later, one very short old lady going up from a small town in Essex, and a very short Catholic priest going up from an Essex village. When it came to this last passenger, Valentin gave up looking and almost laughed. The little priest had a round, dull face; he had eyes as empty as the North Sea; he had several packages wrapped in brown paper, which he was quite unable to hold without dropping one. The meeting of priests in London must have brought out of their quiet villages many similar creatures who seemed blind and helpless, like underground animals dug out of the earth. Even Valentin, who had no love of priests, felt sorry for this one. He had a large, worn suitcase, which kept falling on the floor. He explained to everybody with a kind of foolish simplicity that he had to be careful, because he had something made of real silver 'with blue stones' in one of his brown-paper packages. Watching the priest's confusion continued to amuse the Frenchman until this simple man got out (somehow) at Stratford with all his packages, and came back for his suitcase. When he returned for this, Valentin even had the good nature to warn him not to take care of his silver by telling everybody about it. But whoever he talked to, Valentin watched for someone else: he looked out for anyone, rich or poor, male or female, who was at least six feet tall; for Flambeau was four inches above this height.

He got off the train in central London, though, quite sure that he had not missed the criminal so far. When he had been to Scotland Yard* to arrange for help if it was needed, he went for a long walk in the streets of London. As he was walking in the streets and squares beyond Victoria, he stopped suddenly. He was

* Scotland Yard: the headquarters of the Criminal Investigation Department of London's police force.

in a quiet, attractive square, very typical of London. The tall, flat houses looked both expensive and empty; the gardens in the centre looked as deserted as a green Pacific island. One of the four sides of the square was much higher than the rest, like a stage; and the line of this side was broken by a restaurant. The restaurant stood specially high above the street, and some steps ran up from the street to the front door. Valentin stood and smoked in front of the yellow-white curtains and studied them for a long time.

Aristide Valentin was a thinking man. All his wonderful successes had been gained by slow, patient reasoning, by clear and ordinary French thought. But because Valentin understood reason, he understood its limits. Only a man who knows nothing about cars talks of driving without petrol; only a man who knows nothing of reason talks of reasoning without any hard facts to start with. Flambeau had been missed at Harwich; and if he was in London at all, he might be anything from a tall beggar sleeping in one of the parks to an employee of the Metropole Hotel. When he lacked any such certain knowledge, Valentin had a view and a method of his own.

In such cases he trusted in the unexpected. In such cases, when reasoning was no use to him, he coldly and carefully looked for the unreasonable. Instead of going to the right places – banks, police stations, meeting places – he went to the wrong places; he knocked at every empty house, turned down every little side street, walked up every path. He defended this strange course of action quite reasonably. He said that if he had any facts about the criminal's movements to guide him, this was the worst way; but if he had no facts at all, it was the best. There was just the chance that anything unusual which caught the eye of the hunter might be the same that had caught the eye of the hunted. A man must begin somewhere, and it might as well be just where another man might stop.

Something about the steps leading up to the shop, something about the quiet and rather unusual appearance of the restaurant, gave the detective an idea and made him decide to act without a plan. He went up the steps, sat down by the window and asked for a cup of black coffee. Until his coffee came, he sat thinking about Flambeau. The criminal always had the advantage; he could make his plans and act. The detective could only wait and hope that he would make a mistake.

Valentin lifted his coffee cup to his lips slowly and put it down very quickly. He had put salt in it. He looked at the container from which the white powder had come. It was certainly a sugar bowl. Why had they put salt in it? He looked around for a salt container. Yes, there were two which were quite full. Perhaps there was something unusual about what was in them, too. He tasted it. It was sugar. Then he looked round at the restaurant with new interest, to see if there were any other signs of that strange artistic taste which puts sugar in the salt containers and salt in the sugar bowls. Except for a strange mark of some dark liquid on one of the white walls, the whole place appeared neat, cheerful and ordinary. He rang the bell for the waiter.

When the waiter hurried up to him, his hair uncombed and his eyes rather tired at that early hour, the detective asked him to taste the sugar and see if it was equal to the high standards of the restaurant. The result was that the waiter suddenly woke up.

'Do you play this fine joke on people every morning?' inquired Valentin. 'Do you never grow tired of the joke of changing the salt and the sugar?'

When it became clear to the waiter what Valentin meant, he explained that the restaurant certainly had no such intention; it must be a strange mistake. He picked up the sugar bowl and looked at it; he picked up the salt container and looked at that, his face growing more and more confused. At last he quickly excused himself, hurried away, and returned in a few seconds with the owner of the place. The owner also examined the sugar bowl and then the salt container; the owner also looked confused.

Suddenly the waiter started to speak with a rush of words.

'I think,' he said eagerly, 'I think it was those two priests.'

'What two priests?'

'The two priests,' said the waiter, 'that threw soup at the wall.'

'Threw soup at the wall?' repeated Valentin.

'Yes, yes,' said the waiter with excitement and pointed to the large brown mark on the white wall; 'threw it over there on the wall.'

Valentin looked questioningly at the restaurant owner.

'Yes, sir,' he said, 'it's quite true, although I don't suppose it has anything to do with the sugar and salt. Two priests came in and drank soup here very early, as soon as we opened. They were both very quiet, respectable people. One of them paid the bill and went out; the other, who seemed much slower, was some minutes longer collecting his things together. He went at last. But the moment before he stepped into the street, he deliberately picked up his cup, which he had only half emptied, and threw the soup straight at the wall. I was in the back room myself, and so was the waiter; so I could only rush out in time to find the soup running down the wall and the shop empty. It didn't do any particular damage, but it was a very rude and surprising thing for a priest to do, and I tried to catch the men in the street. They were too far off though; I only noticed that they went round the corner into Carstairs Street.'

The detective was on his feet, with his hat on his head and his stick in his hand. He paid his bill, closed the glass doors loudly behind him, and was soon hurrying round the corner into the next street.

It was fortunate that even in such moments of excitement his eye was cool and quick. Something in a shop window went by him like a flash, but he went back to look at it. It was a fruit and

6

vegetable shop, and the goods were arranged in the open air with tickets on them plainly showing their names and prices. Right in the front were two piles, one of oranges and the other of nuts. On the pile of nuts lay a ticket on which was written clearly: 'Best oranges, two a penny.' On the oranges was the equally clear and exact description: 'Finest nuts, four pence a pound.' Valentin looked at these two tickets and thought that he had experienced this kind of humour before, and that he had done so rather recently. He drew the attention of the red-faced shopkeeper, who seemed in a bad temper and was looking up and down the street, to the mistake in his advertisements. The shopkeeper said nothing, but quickly put each card into its proper place. The detective leaned on his walking stick and continued to look closely at the shop. At last he said, 'Please excuse me, my good sir, but I would like to ask you a question which may sound rather strange.'

The red-faced shopkeeper looked at him threateningly, but the detective continued to lean on his walking stick. 'Why are two tickets wrongly placed in a fruit shop,' he went on, 'like a priest's hat that has come to London for a holiday? Or, in case I do not make myself clear, what is the connection between the idea of nuts marked as oranges and the idea of two priests, one tall and the other short?'

The eyes of the shopkeeper stood out of his head. For a moment he really seemed likely to attack the stranger. At last he said angrily, 'I don't know what you have to do with it. But you can tell them from me that I'll knock their stupid heads off, even if they are priests, if they knock my apples over again.'

'Really?' asked the detective, with great sympathy. 'Did they knock your apples over?'

'One of them did,' said the angry shopkeeper. 'He rolled them all over the street. I would have caught the fool if I hadn't had to pick them up.'

'Which way did these priests go?' asked Valentin.

'Up that second road on the left-hand side, and then across the square,' said the other.

'Thanks,' said Valentin, and moved off quickly. On the other side of the second square he found a policeman, and said, 'This is urgent. Have you seen two priests?'

The policeman began to laugh heavily. 'I have, sir, and if you want my opinion, one of them was drunk. He stood in the middle of the road so confused that—'

'Which way did they go?' interrupted Valentin.

'They took one of those yellow buses over there,' answered the man; 'the ones that go to Hampstead.'

Valentin produced his official card and said very rapidly, 'Call two of your men to come with me to follow these people.' In a minute and a half the French detective was joined on the opposite side of the road by an inspector and a policeman in plain clothes.

'Well, sir,' began the inspector, 'and what may—?'

Valentin pointed suddenly with his stick. 'I'll tell you on the top of that bus,' he said, and ran into the busy traffic. When all three sank, breathing heavily, onto the top seats of the yellow bus, the inspector said: 'We could go four times as quickly in a taxi.'

'Quite true,' replied the leader calmly, 'if we had an idea of where we were going.'

'Well, where *are* you going?' asked the other.

Valentin smoked his cigarette thoughtfully for a few seconds. Then he said, 'If you *know* what a man's doing, get in front of him. But if you want to guess what he's doing, keep behind him. Wander when he wanders; stop when he stops; travel as slowly as he does. Then you can see what he saw, and you can act as he acted. All we can do is to watch very carefully for something unusual.'

'What sort of unusual thing do you mean?' asked the inspector.

'Any sort of unusual thing,' answered Valentin, and became silent.

The yellow bus went slowly up the northern roads for what seemed like hours. The great detective gave no further explanation, and perhaps the other two felt a silent and growing doubt about his purpose. Perhaps, also, they felt a silent and growing desire for lunch, for it was by now long past the normal lunch hour, and the long roads through the north of London seemed to stretch on and on. But even when the winter sun was already beginning to set, the Parisian detective still sat silent and watchful, looking out at the shops and houses that slid by on either side. By the time that they had left Camden Town behind, the policemen were nearly asleep; at least they gave something like a jump as Valentin suddenly stood up, struck each man on the shoulder, and shouted to the driver to stop.

They hurried down the steps and into the road, without knowing why they were doing so. When they looked round for an explanation, they found Valentin pointing his finger in excitement towards a window on the left side of the road. It was a large window, forming part of the long front of a hotel. It was the part for eating in, and was marked 'Restaurant', and in the middle of the window was a big, black hole.

'Our sign at last,' cried Valentin, waving his stick. 'The place with the broken window.'

'What window? What sign?' asked the inspector. 'Why, what proof is there that this has anything to do with them?'

Valentin almost broke his stick in anger.

'Proof!' he cried. 'Good heavens! The man is looking for proof! It is, of course, most unlikely that it has anything to do with them. But what else can we do? Don't you see we must either follow one wild possibility or else go home to bed?' He entered the restaurant with a great deal of noise, followed by his companions, and they were soon eating a late lunch at a little table, and looking at the broken glass from inside. Not that it was very informative to them even then.

'You've had your window broken, I see,' Valentin said to the waiter, as he paid the bill.

'Yes, sir,' the waiter answered. 'A very strange thing that, sir.'

'Really? Tell us about it,' said the detective.

'Well, two gentlemen in black came in,' said the waiter; 'two of those priests that are running around the city at the moment. They had a cheap and quiet little lunch, and one of them paid for it and went out. The other was just going out to join him when I looked at the money he had given me and found that he had paid me more than three times too much. "Here," I said to the priest who was nearly out of the door, "you've paid too much." "Oh," he said, "have we?" "Yes," I said, and I picked up the bill to show him. Well, that was a real surprise.'

'What do you mean?' asked Valentin.

'Well, I could have sworn that I'd put four shillings on that bill. But now I saw quite clearly that I'd put fourteen shillings.'

'Well?' cried Valentin, with burning eyes. 'And then?'

'The priest at the door said quite calmly, "Sorry to confuse your accounts, but it'll pay for the window." "What window?" I said. "The one I'm going to break," he said, and threw a stone through the window.'

The inspector said quietly, 'Are these people completely crazy?'

The waiter continued, obviously enjoying his strange story: 'I was so surprised for a second that I couldn't do anything. The man marched out of the place and joined his friend just round the corner. They went so quickly up Bullock Street that I couldn't catch them.'

'Bullock Street,' said the detective, and ran up that road as quickly as the strange pair that he was following.

Their journey now took them up narrow, brick passages;

streets with few lights and even with few windows. The sun had set further and it was getting dark. It was not easy, even for the London policemen, to guess in what exact direction they were heading. But the inspector was fairly certain that in the end they would reach some part of Hampstead Heath. Suddenly one gas-lit window broke the half-light, and Valentin stopped for a second in front of a small, brightly painted sweet shop. He thought for moment and then went in; he stood among the bright colours of the shop with a serious expression on his face and chose some sweets with great care. He was clearly looking for an opportunity to ask some questions. But this was not necessary.

A thin young woman in the shop had looked at him without interest; but when she saw the door behind him blocked with the blue uniform of the inspector, her eyes seemed to wake up.

'Oh,' she said, 'if you have come about the package, I've sent it off.'

'Package?' repeated Valentin.

'I mean the package the gentleman left – the religious gentleman.'

'Please,' said Valentin, leaning forward eagerly, 'tell us what happened exactly.'

'Well,' said the woman, a little doubtfully, 'the priests came in about half an hour ago and bought some sweets and talked a bit, and then went off towards the Heath. But a second later, one of them ran back into the shop and said, "Have I left a package?" Well, I looked everywhere and couldn't see one; so he said, "Never mind; but if you find it, please post it to this address," and he left me the address and a shilling for my trouble. And then, though I thought I'd looked everywhere, I found he'd left a brown-paper package, so I posted it to the place he said. I can't remember the address now; it was somewhere in Westminster. But as the thing seemed so important, I thought perhaps the police had come about it.'

'So they have,' said Valentin shortly. 'Is Hampstead Heath near here?'

'Straight on for fifteen minutes,' said the woman, 'and you'll come right out on the open ground.' Valentin hurried out of the shop and began to run. The others followed him rather more slowly.

The street that they passed through was so narrow and shut in by shadows that when they suddenly came out into the open park and sky, they were surprised to find the evening still so light and clear. As he stood on the slope and looked across the valley, Valentin saw what he was looking for.

Among the dark groups in the distance was one that was especially dark — two figures dressed as priests. Though they seemed as small as insects, Valentin could see that one of them was much smaller than the other. The other was slightly bent, but was clearly well over six feet tall. Valentin went forward, swinging his stick impatiently. By the time he had shortened the distance and increased the size of the two figures, he had noticed something else; something which surprised him, but which he had somehow expected. Whoever the tall priest was, there could be no doubt who the other one was. It was his friend from the Harwich train, the short little Essex priest whom he had warned about his brown-paper packages.

Now all this was reasonable enough. Valentin had learned from his inquiries that morning that a Father Brown from Essex was bringing up a jewelled silver cross, an ancient object of great value, to show to some of the foreign priests at their meeting in London. This, without any doubt, was the silver cross 'with blue stones'; and Father Brown was undoubtedly the simple little man on the train. Now there was nothing surprising about the fact that what Valentin had found out, Flambeau had also found out; Flambeau found out everything. There was also nothing surprising in the fact that when Flambeau heard of a jewelled cross, he would try to steal it; it was the most natural thing in the world. And most certainly there was nothing surprising about the fact that Flambeau would do as he wished with such a silly sheep as the man with the suitcase and the packages. He was the sort of man whom anybody could lead on a string to the North Pole; it was not surprising that an actor like Flambeau, dressed as another priest, could lead him to Hampstead Heath. So far the crime seemed clear enough; and while the detective pitied the priest for his helplessness, he thought less of Flambeau for choosing such a simple, trusting person to deceive. But when Valentin thought of all that had happened in between, of all that had led him here, he could see no reason in it. What was the connection between the stealing of a jewelled silver cross from a priest from Essex and the throwing of soup at walls? And how were these connected with calling nuts oranges, or with paying for windows first and breaking them afterwards? He had come to the end of his search; but somehow he had missed the middle of it. He had found the criminal, but still could not understand how it had happened.

The two figures that they followed were moving like black flies across the top of a green hill. They were clearly in deep conversation, and perhaps did not notice where they were going; but they were certainly going to the wilder and more silent heights of the Heath. As the policemen came nearer, they had to hide behind trees and even to go along on their hands and knees in deep grass to remain invisible. By these means the hunters even came close enough to the priests to hear the sound of their discussion, but no word could be clearly heard and understood except the word 'reason', which was spoken frequently in a high and almost childish voice. Once, over a sudden rise in the ground and in thick bushes, the detectives actually lost the two figures that they were following. They did not find the right path again for an anxious ten minutes, and then it led round the top of a great round hill overlooking a wide hollow of rich, empty sunset scenery. Under a tree in this beautiful but lonely spot was an old wooden seat. On this seat sat the two priests, still talking seriously to each other. Valentin signalled silently to his followers and moved forward to hide behind a big branching tree, where, hardly breathing, he heard the words of the strange priests for the first time.

After he had listened for a minute and a half, he experienced a terrible doubt. For the two priests were talking exactly like priests, talking calmly and knowledgeably about religion. The little Essex priest spoke more simply, with his round face turned to the brightening stars; the other talked with his face to the ground, as if he were not fit to look at them. But no more priest-like conversation could have been heard.

The first he heard was the end of one of Father Brown's sentences, which was: '. . . what they really meant in the Middle Ages by the heavens being unchanging and unchangeable.'

The taller priest replied: 'Ah, yes, who can look up at those millions of worlds and not feel that there may well be wonderful universes above us where reason is quite unreasonable?'

Valentin behind his tree was tearing his fingernails with silent anger. He could almost hear the quiet laughter of the English detectives whom he had brought so far on a wild guess only to listen to the talk of two old priests. When he listened again, it was again Father Brown who was speaking.

'Look at those stars. Don't they look like diamonds? But don't imagine that all that study of heavenly bodies would make the slightest difference to the reason and justice of behaviour. In fields of jewels, under hills cut from gold, you would still find a notice saying "You must not steal".'

Valentin was just about to rise from his stiff and bent position and to move away as quietly as he could, but something in the silence of the tall priest made him stop until this man spoke. When at last he did speak, he said simply, his head still lowered

14

and his hands on his knees: 'Well, I still think that other worlds may perhaps rise higher than our reason. The mystery of heaven cannot be understood, and I myself can only bend my head in respect.'

Then, with his head still bent forward, and without the slightest change in expression, he added: 'Just give me that cross of yours, will you? We're all alone here, and I could pull you to pieces like a child's toy.'

The completely unchanged voice and attitude added a strange violence to that shocking change of speech. But the little priest only seemed to turn his head by the smallest degree. He seemed still to have a rather foolish face turned to the stars. Perhaps he had not understood. Or perhaps he had understood and sat frozen with fear.

'Yes,' said the tall priest, in the same low voice and with his head still low, 'yes, I am Flambeau.'

Then, after a pause, he said: 'Now, will you give me that cross?'

'No,' said the other, and the word had a strange sound.

Flambeau suddenly stopped pretending to be a priest. The great robber leaned back in his seat and laughed quietly, but for a long time.

'No,' he cried; 'you won't give it to me, you simple fool. Shall I tell you why you won't give it to me? Because I've got it already in my pocket.'

The small man from Essex turned towards him what seemed, in the half-light, to be a confused face and said carefully: 'Are – are you sure?'

Flambeau shouted with pleasure.

'Really, you are amusing!' he cried. 'Yes, you fool, I am quite sure. I had the sense to make a copy of the real package, and now, my friend, you've got the copy, and I've got the jewels. An old trick, Father Brown – a very old trick.'

'Yes,' said Father Brown, and passed his hand through his hair in the same strange confused manner. 'Yes, I've heard of it before.'

The great criminal leaned over to the little country priest with a sort of sudden interest.

'*You* have heard of it?' he asked. 'Where have *you* heard of it?'

'Well, I mustn't tell you his name, of course,' said the little man simply. 'He was a man who had come back to the Church after a life of crime. He lived very comfortably for about twenty years on copies of brown-paper packages. And so, you see, when I began to suspect you, I thought immediately of this poor man's way of doing it.'

'Began to suspect me?' repeated the criminal. 'Did you really have the sense to suspect me just because I brought you up to this lonely part of the Heath?'

'No, no,' said Brown, with a faint smile. 'You see, I suspected you when we first met. It's the shape of the gun showing under your coat.'

'How,' cried Flambeau, 'did you notice that? It's supposed to be invisible.'

'Oh, one's work, you know!' said Father Brown. 'When I was a priest in Hartlepool, I knew quite a number of people who always carried guns. So, as I suspected you from the start, I made sure that the cross would be safe. I'm afraid I watched you, you know. So I saw you change the packages. Then I changed them back again. And then I left the right one behind.'

'Left it behind?' repeated Flambeau, and for the first time there was another note in his voice beside victory.

'Well, it was like this,' said the priest, speaking in the same simple way. 'I went back to the sweet shop and asked if I'd left a package, and gave them a particular address if it was found. Well, I knew that I hadn't; but when I went away again I did. So instead of running after me with that valuable package, they have sent it by post to a friend of mine in Westminster.' He added rather sadly: 'I learned that, too, from a poor man in Hartlepool. He used to do it with handbags that he stole at railway stations, but he's a good man now. One gets to know, you know,' he added, rubbing his head. 'We can't help it, being priests. People come and tell us these things.'

Flambeau pulled a brown-paper package out of his pocket and tore it open. There was nothing but paper and pencils inside. He jumped to his feet and cried: 'I don't believe you. I don't believe that a simple fool like you could manage all that. I believe that you've still got the cross with you, and if you don't give it up – well, we're all alone, and I'll take it by force!'

'No,' said Father Brown simply, standing up too; 'you won't take it by force. First, because I really haven't still got it. And, second, because we're not alone.'

Flambeau stopped in his step forward.

'Behind that tree,' said Father Brown, pointing, 'are two strong policemen and the greatest detective alive. How did they come here, do you ask? Well, I brought them, of course! We have to know about such things when we work among the criminal classes! Well, I wasn't sure you were a thief, and it would not be right to charge one of our own priests. So I just tested you to see if anything would make you show yourself. A man usually complains if he finds salt in his coffee; if he doesn't, he has some reason for keeping quiet. I changed the salt and sugar, and you kept quiet. A man generally objects if his bill is three times too big. If he pays it, he has some reason for passing unnoticed. I changed your bill and you paid it.

'Well,' went on Father Brown, 'as you weren't leaving any tracks for the police, of course somebody had to. At every place we went to, I took care to do something that would get us talked about for the rest of the day. I didn't do much harm – a dirty wall, apples in the street, a broken window; but I saved the cross, as the cross will always be saved. It is in Westminster by now.'

'How on earth did you think of these things?' cried Flambeau.

The shadow of a smile crossed the round, simple face of his opponent.

'Oh, by being a foolish priest, I suppose,' he said. 'Have you never thought that a man who does almost nothing except listen to men talking about their crimes is likely to know a little of human evil?'

And as he turned to collect his property, the three policemen came out from under the dark trees. Flambeau was an artist and a sportsman. He raised his hat to Valentin as a respectful greeting.

'Do not raise your hat to me, my friend,' said Valentin in a clear voice. 'Let us both raise our hats to our master.'

And they both stood for a moment with their hats in their hands, while the little Essex priest looked around for his suitcase.

Philomel Cottage   *Agatha Christie*

'Goodbye, my love.'

'Goodbye, dearest.'

Alix Martin leaned over the small garden gate and watched the figure of her husband grow smaller as he walked down the road in the direction of the village.

Soon he turned a bend and disappeared, but Alix still stayed in the same position, with a dreamy, faraway look in her eyes.

Alix Martin was not beautiful. She was not even particularly pretty, but there was a joy and softness in her face which her friends from the past would not have recognized. Alix had not had an easy life. For fifteen years, from the age of eighteen until she was thirty-three, she had had to look after herself (and for seven years of that time her sick mother as well). She had worked as a secretary, and she had been neat and businesslike. But the struggle had brought lines to her young face.

It was true that she had had a sort of love affair – with Dick Windyford, another clerk. Although they had seemed to be just good friends, Alix knew in her heart that he loved her. But Dick had to work hard in order to save enough money to send a younger brother to a good school. He could not think of marriage yet.

Then, suddenly, the girl was delivered from the dullness of her everyday life in the most surprising manner. A cousin died and left all her money, a few thousand pounds, to Alix. This gave Alix freedom, an easier life and the ability to make her own decisions. Now she and Dick did not need to wait any longer to be married.

But Dick behaved strangely. He had never spoken directly to Alix of his love for her, and now he seemed to have less desire than ever to do so. He avoided her, and became silent and unhappy. Alix was quick to realize the truth. She had become a wealthy woman, and Dick's pride would not allow him to ask her to be his wife.

She liked him none the worse for it and was actually thinking about suggesting marriage herself, when the second surprising thing happened to her.

She met Gerald Martin at a friend's house. He fell violently in love with her, and within a week he had asked her to marry him. Alix, who had always considered herself calm and sensible, was completely swept off her feet.

She had, by chance, found a way to excite Dick Windyford's emotions. He had come to her almost speechless with anger.

'The man's a complete stranger to you! You know nothing about him!'

'I know that I love him.'

'How can you know – in a week?'

'It doesn't take everyone eleven years to find out that they're in love with a girl,' cried Alix angrily.

His face went white. 'I've loved you ever since I met you. I thought that you felt the same about me.'

Alix was truthful. 'I thought so too,' she admitted. 'But that was because I didn't know what real love was.'

Then Dick had exploded again, shouting first prayers and then threats – threats against the man who had taken his place. Alix was shocked to see how strong the feelings were of the man whom she had thought that she knew so well.

As she leaned on the gate of the little house on this sunny morning, her thoughts went back to that conversation. She had been married for a month, and she was wonderfully happy. But now and again there were moments of anxiety which darkened her perfect happiness. And the cause of that anxiety was Dick Windyford. Three times since her marriage she had dreamed the same dream. Although the place was different on each occasion, the main facts were always the same. *She saw her husband lying dead and Dick Windyford standing over him, and she knew quite clearly that it was Dick who had struck him down.*

But if that was terrible, there was something more terrible still, although in the dream it seemed completely natural. *She, Alix Martin, was glad that her husband was dead*; she stretched out grateful hands to the murderer, and sometimes she thanked him. The dream always ended in the same way, with herself held in Dick Windyford's arms.

She had said nothing about this dream to her husband, but secretly it troubled her more than she liked to admit. Was it a warning – a warning against Dick Windyford?

Alix was woken from her thoughts by the sharp sound of the telephone ringing in the house. She went inside and picked up the receiver. Suddenly she felt faint and put out a hand against the wall.

'Who did you say was speaking?'

'Why, Alix, what's the matter with your voice? I hardly recognized it. It's Dick.'

'Oh!' said Alix. 'Oh! Where – where are you?'

'At the Traveller's Arms – that's the right name, isn't it? Or don't you even know of the existence of your village inn? I'm on holiday and doing a bit of fishing here. Would you have any objections if I came to see you both this evening after dinner?'

'No,' said Alix sharply. 'You mustn't come.'

There was a pause, and then Dick spoke again. 'I beg your pardon,' he said formally. 'Of course I won't trouble you–'

Alix interrupted quickly. He must think that her behaviour was strange, and it was.

'I only meant to say that we are – busy tonight,' she explained, trying to make her voice sound as natural as possible. 'Will you – will you come to dinner tomorrow night?'

But Dick had noticed the lack of warmth in her voice.

'Thanks very much,' he said, as formally as before, 'but I may leave at any time. I'm expecting to be joined by a friend. Goodbye, Alix.' He paused, and then added quickly, with his old friendliness: 'Best of luck to you, my dear.'

Alix put the phone down with a feeling of relief.

'He mustn't come here,' she repeated to herself. 'He mustn't come here. Oh, what a fool I am to get into a state like this! But even so, I'm glad that he's not coming.'

She picked up an old hat from a table and went out into the garden again, pausing to look up at the name which was cut into the stone above the front door: Philomel★ Cottage.

'It's a strange name, isn't it?' she had said to Gerald once before they were married. He had laughed.

'You little town girl,' he had said lovingly. 'I don't believe that you've ever heard a nightingale. I'm glad that you haven't. Nightingales should only sing for lovers. We'll hear them together on a summer's evening outside our own home.'

And when Alix, standing in the doorway of their home, remembered how they had heard them, she smiled happily.

It was Gerald who had found Philomel Cottage. He had come to Alix full of excitement about it. He told her that he had found the perfect house for them – a real jewel of a place. And when Alix had seen it she, too, fell in love with it. It was true that it was in rather a lonely position – it was two miles from the nearest village – but the house itself was wonderful. It was attractive to look at, and it had a comfortable bathroom, a good hot-water system, electric light and telephone. But then they had a great disappointment. Gerald found out that the owner, although a rich man, would not rent it to them. He would only sell it.

Gerald Martin had plenty of family money, but he was only

★ Philomel: the poetic name for the nightingale.

able to use the income from it. He could lay his hands on no more than a thousand pounds. The owner wanted three thousand. But Alix, who had set her heart on the house, suddenly stepped in. She gave half of her money in order to buy the home. So Philomel Cottage had become their own, and Alix had not felt for a minute that she had made the wrong choice. It was true that servants did not like the loneliness of the country – actually, at the moment they had none at all – but Alix, who had had little home life before, thoroughly enjoyed cooking lovely meals and looking after the house. The garden, which was well stocked with the most beautiful flowers, was cared for by an old man from the village who came twice a week.

As she turned the corner of the house, Alix was surprised to see the old gardener busy in the flowerbeds. She was surprised because his days for work were Mondays and Fridays, and today was Wednesday.

'What are you doing here, George?' she asked, as she came towards him.

'I thought that you'd be surprised. But there's a country show near here on Friday, so I said to myself that neither Mr Martin nor his good wife would mind if I came for once on a Wednesday instead of a Friday.'

'That's quite all right,' said Alix. 'I hope that you'll enjoy yourself at the show.'

'I intend to,' said George simply. 'But I did think, too, that I'd see you before you went away to find out what you want me to do with the flower borders. You haven't any idea when you'll be back, I suppose?'

'But I'm not going away.'

George looked at her in surprise. 'Aren't you going to London tomorrow?'

'No. What gave you such an idea?'

'I met master going down to the village yesterday. He told me

23

that you were both going away to London tomorrow, and that it was uncertain when you'd be back again.'

'Nonsense,' said Alix, laughing. 'You must have misunderstood him.'

Just the same, it made her think about exactly what Gerald could have said for the old man to make such a strange mistake. Going to London? She never wanted to go to London again.

'I hate London,' she said suddenly and bitterly.

'Ah!' said George calmly. 'I must have been mistaken somehow, but he said it quite plainly, it seemed to me. I'm glad that you're staying here. I don't approve of all this moving about, and I don't like London at all. *I've* never needed to go there. Too many motor cars – that's the trouble these days. As soon as people have got a motor car, they can't seem to stay still anywhere. Mr Ames, who used to have this cottage, was a nice peaceful gentleman until he bought one of those things. He hadn't had it a month before he put this cottage up for sale. He'd spent a lot of money on it, too, putting in electric light and things like that. "You'll never get your money back," I said to him. "But," he said to me, "I'll get two thousand pounds for this house." And he certainly did.'

'He got three thousand,' said Alix, smiling.

'Two thousand,' repeated George. 'There was talk at the time about the amount that he wanted.'

'It really was three thousand,' said Alix.

'Ladies never understand figures,' said George firmly. 'You're not going to tell me that Mr Ames asked you for three thousand?'

'He didn't ask me,' said Alix; 'he asked my husband.'

George bent down again to his flowerbed.

'The price was two thousand,' he said with determination.

Alix did not argue with him any more. She moved across to one of the other beds and began to pick a bunch of flowers.

As she moved towards the house, Alix noticed a small, dark green object lying on the ground. She stopped and picked it up, recognizing it as her husband's notebook.

She opened it and looked rapidly through it with some amusement. Almost from the beginning of her married life with Gerald she had realized that, although he was quick and emotional, he was also unexpectedly neat and well organized. He demanded that his meals were served on time and always planned his day with great care.

As she looked through the notebook Alix smiled to see the entry for 14th May: 'Marry Alix St Peter's 2.30.' She laughed, and turned the pages. Suddenly she stopped.

'"Wednesday, 18th June" – that's today.'

In the space for that day, Gerald had written in his neat, exact hand: '9 p.m.' Nothing else. What did Gerald plan to do at 9 p.m.? Alix thought about it. She smiled to herself as she realized that if this had been a detective story, the notebook would have contained some unpleasant surprises. One of them would certainly have been the name of another woman. She turned back the pages carelessly. There were dates, appointments, short notes on business matters, but only one woman's name – her own.

But as she slipped the book into her pocket and carried her flowers into the house, she felt a slight anxiety. She remembered Dick Windyford's words almost as though he were beside her repeating them: 'The man's a complete stranger to you. You know nothing about him.'

It was true. What did she know about him? After all, Gerald was forty. In forty years there must have been other women in his life . . .

Alix shook herself impatiently. She must not think like this. She had a more urgent matter to deal with. Ought she or ought she not to tell her husband that Dick Windyford had telephoned her?

It was just possible that Gerald had already met him in the

village. But in that case he would be sure to mention it to her immediately on his return, and she could then safely tell him about the phone call. If he did not – what? Alix felt a strong desire to say nothing about it.

If she told him, he was sure to suggest that they should invite Dick Windyford to Philomel Cottage. Then she would have to explain that Dick had asked if he could come, and that she had made an excuse to prevent him. And when he asked her why she had done so, what could she say? Should she tell him her dream? But he would only laugh – or, to make matters worse, he would see that she thought it was important.

In the end, although she felt rather ashamed, Alix decided to say nothing. It was the first secret that she had ever kept from her husband, and she felt very uncomfortable about it.

♦

When she heard Gerald returning from the village at lunchtime, Alix hid her confusion by hurrying into the kitchen and pretending to be busy with the cooking.

She realized immediately that Gerald had not seen Dick Windyford. She was relieved, but she remained a little anxious because she had to prevent Gerald from learning what had happened.

It was not until they had finished their simple evening meal and were sitting in the living room, with the windows open in order to let in the sweet night air and the smell of the flowers, that Alix remembered the notebook.

'Here's something that you've been watering the flowers with,' she said, and threw it to him.

'I dropped it in the flowerbed, did I?'

'Yes; I know all your secrets now.'

'Not guilty,' said Gerald, shaking his head.

'What about your secret business at nine o'clock tonight?'

26

'Oh, that . . . !' He seemed surprised for a moment, and then he smiled as if he had had a particularly amusing thought. 'It's a meeting with a specially nice girl, Alix. She's got brown hair and blue eyes and she's very like you.'

'I don't understand,' said Alix, pretending to be severe. 'You're avoiding the point.'

'No, I'm not. As a matter of fact, it's a note to remind myself that I'm going to develop some photographs tonight, and I want you to help me.'

Gerald Martin was very interested in photography and had an excellent, but rather old camera. He developed his photographs in a small room under the house, which he had fitted up for that purpose.

'And the developing must be done at nine o'clock exactly,' said Alix, laughing.

Gerald looked a little annoyed.

'My dear girl,' he said, 'one should always plan a thing for a certain time. Then one does one's work quickly and properly.'

Alix sat for a minute or two in silence, watching her husband. He sat back in his chair smoking, with his dark head leaning back and the clear-cut lines of his face standing out against the dark background. And suddenly Alix felt a wave of fear sweep over her, so that she cried out before she could stop herself: 'Oh, Gerald, I wish that I knew more about you!'

Her husband looked at her in surprise.

'But my dear Alix, you do know all about me. I've told you about when I was a boy in Northumberland, about my life in South Africa, and about these last ten years in Canada which have made me successful.'

'Oh, business!' said Alix, with a wave of her hand to show her lack of interest.

Gerald laughed suddenly. 'I know what you mean – love affairs. You women are all the same.'

Alix felt her throat go dry, as she said nervously: 'Well, but there must have been – love affairs – if I only knew . . .'

There was silence again for a minute or two. Gerald Martin looked worried and undecided. When he spoke, he spoke seriously, without any sign of his former light-hearted manner.

'Alix, do you think that it's wise to want to know so much? Yes, there have been women in my life. If I said there were not, you wouldn't believe me. But I can swear to you that not one of them was important to me.'

His voice was so sincere that Alix was comforted.

'Are you satisfied, Alix?' he asked with a smile. 'What's made you think of this tonight especially?'

Alix got up and began to walk about the room.

'Oh, I don't know,' she said. 'I've been feeling anxious all day.'

'That's strange,' said Gerald in a low voice, as though he was speaking to himself. 'That's very strange.'

'Why is it strange?'

'Oh, my dear girl, don't turn on me like that. I only said that it was strange because as a rule you're so happy and cheerful.'

Alix forced herself to smile.

'Everything's done its best to annoy me today,' she admitted. 'Even old George had got hold of some strange idea that we were going away to London. He said that you had told him so.'

'Where did you see him?' asked Gerald sharply.

'He came to work today instead of Friday.'

'The stupid old fool,' said Gerald angrily.

Alix looked at him in surprise. Her husband's face was twisted with violent anger. She had never seen him like this. When Gerald noticed her shocked expression, he made an effort to regain control of himself.

'Well, he *is* a stupid old fool,' he complained.

'What can you have said to make him think that?'

'I? I never said anything. At least – oh, yes, I remember; I made

28

some weak joke about going "off to London in the morning", and I suppose that he believed me. Or perhaps he didn't hear me properly. You corrected him, of course?'

He waited anxiously for her reply.

'Of course, but he's the sort of old man who doesn't accept correction easily.'

She told him how certain George had been about the price of the house.

Gerald was silent for a minute or two, then he said slowly: 'Ames was prepared to take two thousand pounds immediately and to be paid the remaining one thousand in small amounts over several months. That's how that mistake started, I expect.'

'Very likely,' Alix agreed.

Then she looked up at the clock, and pointed to it with a laugh.

'We ought to be getting on with the developing, Gerald. It's five past nine.'

A very strange smile appeared on Gerald Martin's face.

'I've changed my mind,' he said quietly. 'I shan't do any photography tonight.'

♦

A woman's mind is a strange thing. When Alix went to bed on that Wednesday night, her mind was as peaceful and happy as it had been before Dick Windyford's phone call.

But by the evening of the following day she was feeling anxious again. Dick had not telephoned again, but she felt what she supposed must be his influence at work. Again and again she seemed to hear those words of his: '*The man's a complete stranger to you. You know nothing about him.*'

And with them came the memory of her husband's face and the way that he had said, 'Alix, do you think that it's wise to want to know so much?' Why had he said that? There had been a warning in those words. It was as though he had said, 'You had better not try to find out about my past life, Alix. You may get an unpleasant shock if you do.'

By Friday morning Alix felt certain that there *had* been a woman in Gerald's life – and that he had taken great care to hide the fact from her. Her jealousy, which had developed slowly, now became violent.

Was it a woman that he had been going to meet that night at 9 p.m.? When he had said that he had been planning to develop photographs, had he been lying?

Three days ago she would have sworn that she knew her husband completely. Now it seemed to her that he was in fact a stranger to her. She remembered his unreasonable anger against old George, which had been so different from his usual good temper. Perhaps it was a small thing, but it showed her that she did not really know the man who was her husband.

On Friday afternoon there were several little things that Alix needed from the village. She suggested that she should go and buy them while Gerald remained in the garden; but rather to her surprise he objected strongly to this plan, and stated that he would go himself while she remained at home. Alix was forced to give way to him, but his determination surprised and worried her. Why was he so anxious to prevent her from going to the village?

Suddenly she thought of an explanation which made the whole thing clear. Was it not possible that, although he had said nothing to her, Gerald actually had met Dick Windyford? Her own jealousy had only developed since her marriage. The same thing might have happened with Gerald. He might be anxious to prevent her from seeing Dick Windyford again. This explanation fitted the facts so well, and was so comforting to Alix's troubled mind, that she accepted it eagerly.

But by teatime she was again feeling uncomfortable. She was

struggling with an idea that, to her shame, had come to her since Gerald left. At last, after she had told herself repeatedly that she ought to tidy Gerald's dressing room, she went upstairs. She took a duster with her to pretend that she was just being a good housewife.

'If I was only sure,' she repeated to herself. 'If I could only be *sure*.'

She tried to believe that Gerald would have destroyed anything to do with a woman in his past life. But the desire to find out for herself grew stronger and stronger, until at last she could no longer stop herself. Although she felt deeply ashamed of herself, she searched the drawers, hunting through packets of letters and papers and even the pockets of her husband's clothes. Only two drawers escaped her: the lower drawer of the dressing table and the small right-hand drawer of the writing desk were both locked. But Alix had by now lost all her shame. She was certain that in one of those drawers she would find something connected with this imaginary woman from the past who was driving her crazy.

She remembered that Gerald had left his keys lying carelessly on the table downstairs. She brought them upstairs and tried them one by one. The third key fitted the drawer of the writing desk. Alix pulled it open eagerly. There was a chequebook and some money in there, and at the back of the drawer a packet of letters tied up with a piece of string.

Alix was breathing unsteadily as she untied the string. Then her face turned red and she dropped the letters back into the drawer, closing and relocking it. The letters were her own, which she had written to Gerald Martin before she married him.

Then she turned to the dressing table. She did not expect to find what she was looking for, but she wanted to feel that she had not left the search unfinished.

Alix was annoyed to find that none of the keys in Gerald's

bunch fitted this particular drawer. But she was determined not to be defeated. She went round the other rooms in the house and brought back a collection of keys with her; finally she discovered that the key of the cupboard in another room also fitted the drawers of the dressing table. She unlocked the lower drawer and pulled it open. But there was nothing in it except a roll of old and dirty newspaper cuttings.

Alix breathed more freely. But she looked quickly at the cuttings, because she was interested to know what subject had interested Gerald so much that he had kept them. They were nearly all from American newspapers of about seven years before, and they dealt with the trial of Charles Lemaitre. Lemaitre had been suspected of marrying women in order to murder them for their money. A skeleton had been found beneath the floor of one of the houses which he had rented, and most of the women that he had 'married' had never been heard of again.

He had defended himself in court with the greatest skill, and had been helped by some of the best lawyers in the United States. The court had been unable to prove the main charge of murder, but had found him guilty of several smaller charges, and he had been put in prison.

Alix remembered the excitement caused by the case at the time, and again some three years later when Lemaitre had escaped from prison. He had never been caught. The English newspapers had discussed at great length the character of the man and his strange power over women; they had described his excitable behaviour in court, and mentioned the occasional sudden illnesses caused by his heart condition.

There was a picture of him in one of the cuttings and Alix looked closely at it. It showed a thoughtful, bearded gentleman.

Who was it that the face reminded her of? Suddenly, with a shock, she realized that it was Gerald himself. The eyes were just like his. Perhaps he had kept the cutting for that reason. She

32

began to read the account beside the picture. It seemed that certain dates had been written in Lemaitre's notebook, and it was suggested that these were the dates on which the women had been murdered. In court, a witness had stated that Lemaitre could be recognized by the mark of an old injury on the inside of his left wrist.

Alix dropped the papers and put out a hand to support herself. *Her husband had a mark on the inside of his left wrist . . .*

The room seemed to spin around her. Gerald Martin was Charles Lemaitre! She knew it and accepted it in a flash. Unconnected facts suddenly fitted together.

The money that had been paid for the house was all hers, and she had trusted him with the rest of her money. Even her dream now had a meaning. Deep down, although she had never consciously known it, she had always feared Gerald Martin. She had wished to escape from him, and had unconsciously wanted Dick Windyford's help. That, too, was why she had accepted the truth so easily, without doubt or further thought. Lemaitre had meant to kill her too. Very soon, perhaps . . .

She almost cried out as she remembered something. *Wednesday 9 p.m.* The room under the house, with the floor-stones which could be raised so easily! Once before he had buried a body under a floor. It had all been planned for Wednesday night. But was he crazy, writing down the date and time in his notebook? No. Gerald always wrote down his business appointments: to him, murder was a form of business.

But what had saved her? What could possibly have saved her? Had he changed his mind at the last minute? No. She realized immediately – *old George.*

She understood now her husband's burst of uncontrollable anger.

No doubt he had prepared the way by telling as many people as possible that they were going to London the next day. Then

33

George had come to work unexpectedly. He had mentioned London to her and she had said that the story was untrue. It would have been too risky to murder her that night, if old George was likely to repeat that conversation. But what an escape! If she had not happened to mention that little matter – Alix trembled.

But she had no time to waste. She must get away immediately – before he came back. She quickly replaced the roll of cuttings in the drawer, shut it and locked it.

And then she froze. She heard the noise of the garden gate. *Her husband had returned.*

For a moment Alix did not move; then she walked softly to the window and looked out from behind the shelter of the curtain.

Yes, it was her husband. He was smiling to himself and singing a little song. He held in his hand an object which almost stopped the beating of her heart. It was a new spade.

Alix understood immediately. *It would be tonight . . .*

But there was still a chance. Gerald, still singing, went round to the back of the house.

She didn't wait. She ran down the stairs and out of the house. But just as she came out of the front door, her husband reappeared round the other side of the house.

'Hello,' he said, 'where are you running off to in such a hurry?'

Alix did her best to remain as calm as usual. Her opportunity had gone for the moment but it would come again later if she took care not to make him suspicious. Even now, perhaps . . .

'I was going to walk to the end of the road and back,' she said in a voice which sounded weak and uncertain to her own ears.

'All right,' said Gerald, 'I'll come with you.'

'No, please, Gerald. I'm not feeling too well – I'd rather go alone.'

He looked at her closely. She thought she saw a flash of suspicion in his eyes.

34

'What's the matter with you, Alix? You're pale, and you're shaking.'

'Nothing.' She forced herself to smile and sound confident. 'I've got a headache, that's all. A walk will do me good.'

'Well, it's no good your saying that you don't want me,' said Gerald, laughing. 'I'm coming, whether you want me or not.'

She did not dare object any more. If he suspected that she *knew* . . .

With an effort she managed to regain something of her normal manner. But she had an uncomfortable feeling that he was looking at her every now and then out of the corner of his eye, as if his suspicions had still not completely disappeared.

When they returned to the house he made her lie down, and he cared for her like any loving husband. Alix felt as helpless as if she was in a trap with her hands and feet tied.

He would not leave her alone for a minute. He went with her to the kitchen and helped her to bring in the simple cold dishes which she had already prepared. She knew now that she was fighting for her life. She was alone with this man, help was miles away and she was completely in his power. Her only chance was to calm his suspicions so that he would leave her alone for long enough to reach the telephone in the hall and call for help. That was her only hope now.

She had a moment of hope as she remembered how he had given up his plan before. She was on the point of telling him that Dick Windyford was coming up to see them that evening, but she realized that this would be useless. The murderer would not be stopped a second time. There was a determination in his calm behaviour that made her feel sick with fear. He would simply murder her immediately and telephone Dick Windyford with a story that they had been called away suddenly. Oh, if Dick Windyford would come to the house this evening! If Dick . . .

A sudden idea came to her mind. She looked sharply at her

husband, as though she was afraid that he would understand what was in her mind. Now that she had formed a plan, her courage returned and she was able to behave naturally again.

She made the coffee, and they took it outside as they always did when it was a fine evening.

'Oh, yes,' said Gerald suddenly, 'we'll do those photographs later.'

Alix's blood seemed to go cold, but she simply replied, 'Can't you manage alone? I'm rather tired tonight.'

'It won't take long.' He smiled to himself. 'And I can promise you that you won't feel tired afterwards.'

The words seemed to amuse him. Alix closed her eyes. She had to carry out her plan now.

'I'm just going to telephone the butcher,' she told him.

'The butcher? At this time of night?'

'Oh, of course his shop's shut. But I can ring him at home. Tomorrow is Saturday and I forgot to ask him to bring me some meat for the weekend. The dear old man will do anything for me.'

She passed quickly into the house, closing the door behind her. She heard Gerald say, 'Don't shut the door,' and replied cheerfully, 'Are you afraid that I'm going to make love to the butcher?'

As soon as she was inside, she picked up the phone and asked for the number of the Traveller's Arms. She was connected immediately.

'Mr Windyford? Is he still there? Can I speak to him?'

Then her heart began to beat more quickly. The door was opened and her husband came into the hall.

'Do go away, Gerald,' she said angrily. 'I hate anyone to listen when I'm telephoning.'

He just laughed and sat down in a chair.

'Are you sure it's really the butcher that you're telephoning?' he laughed.

Alix now felt real terror. Her plan had failed. In a minute Dick Windyford would come to the phone. Should she take a risk and cry out for help?

In her anxiety she began to press one of the buttons on the phone up and down, and immediately another plan flashed into her head. When the button was pressed down, the voice could not be heard at the other end, but when it was up, it could.

'It will be difficult,' she thought to herself. 'I must keep calm, think of the right words and not pause for a moment, but I believe that I can do it. I *must* do it.'

And at that minute she heard Dick Windyford's voice at the other end of the line.

Alix took a deep breath. Then she spoke.

'*Mrs Martin speaking — from Philomel Cottage. Please come* (she pushed the button) tomorrow morning with a good cut of lamb for two people (button up). *It's very important* (button down). Thank you so much, Mr Hexworthy; I hope that you don't mind me ringing up so late, but the meat is really a matter of (button up) *life or death* (button down). Very well — tomorrow morning (button up) *as soon as possible.*'

She replaced the receiver and faced her husband, breathing hard.

'So that's how you talk to your butcher, is it?' said Gerald.

'It's a woman's touch,' said Alix lightly.

She was shaking with excitement. He had suspected nothing. Dick would come, even if he didn't understand.

She walked into the sitting room and switched on the light. Gerald followed her.

'You seem to be in very high spirits now,' he said, watching her with interest.

'Yes,' said Alix. 'My headache's gone.'

She sat down in her usual seat and smiled at her husband as he sank into his own chair opposite her. She was saved. It was only twenty-five minutes past eight. Dick would arrive long before nine o'clock.

'I didn't like the coffee that you gave me very much,' Gerald complained. 'It tasted very bitter.'

'It's a new kind that I was trying. We won't have it again if you don't like it, dear.'

Alix picked up some sewing. Gerald read a few pages of his book. Then he looked up at the clock and put it away.

'Half past eight. It's time to go downstairs and start work.'

The sewing slipped from Alix's fingers.

'Oh, not yet. Let's wait until nine o'clock.'

'No, my girl – half past eight. That's the time that I fixed. You'll be able to go to bed earlier.'

'But I'd rather wait until nine.'

'You know that when I fix a time, I always keep to it. Come along, Alix. I'm not going to wait a minute longer.'

Alix looked up at him. His hands were shaking and his eyes shining with excitement, and his tongue kept moving across his dry lips. He no longer tried to hide his eagerness.

Alix thought, 'It's true – *he can't wait* – he really is crazy.'

He seized her by the shoulder and pulled her to her feet.

'Come on my girl – or I'll carry you there.'

He spoke brightly, but there was a power in his voice that was terrible. With a great effort she pushed him away and pressed herself back against the wall. She was helpless. She couldn't get away – she couldn't do anything – and he was coming towards her.

'Now, Alix–'

'No – no.' She cried out loud, trying hopelessly to keep him away with her hands.

'Gerald – stop – there's something I've got to tell you, something important . . .'

He did stop.

'Important?' he said with interest. Then a look of anger appeared on his face. 'A former lover, I suppose?'

'No,' said Alix. 'Something else. I expect that you'd call it – yes, you'd call it a crime.'

She immediately saw that she had said the right thing. His attention was held. As soon as she realized this, her courage returned to her. She felt that she was in control of the situation again.

'You'd better sit down again,' she said quietly.

She herself crossed the room to her old chair and sat down. She even bent down and picked up her sewing. But behind her calmness she was feverishly inventing a story that would hold his interest until help arrived.

'I told you,' she said slowly, 'that I had been a secretary for fifteen years. That was not completely true. I was not a secretary for all of that time. When I was twenty-two, I met a man, a fairly old man, with a little property. He fell in love with me and asked me to marry him. I accepted. We were married.' She paused. 'I persuaded him to insure his life in my name.'

She saw a sudden look of interest appear on her husband's face, and she went on with increased confidence.

'During the war I worked for a time in a hospital. There I handled all kinds of rare poisons.'

There was no doubt that Gerald was extremely interested now. A murderer is sure to have an interest in murder. She had taken a chance on that, and succeeded. She looked quickly at the clock. It was twenty-five minutes to nine.

'There is one poison – it is a little white powder – of which just a very small amount causes death. You know something about poisons perhaps?'

She put the question with some anxiety. If he did, she would have to be careful.

'No,' said Gerald. 'I know very little about them.'

39

She was greatly relieved.

'You have probably heard of a poison called hyoscine? The poison that I am speaking of acts in the same sort of way, but afterwards it is impossible to find any sign of it in the body. A doctor would believe that the heart had failed. I stole a small quantity of this poison and kept it.'

She stopped.

'Go on,' said Gerald.

'No. I'm afraid. I can't tell you. Another time.'

'Now,' he said impatiently. 'I want to hear.'

'We'd been married for a month. I was very good to my old husband, and since he praised me to all the neighbours, everyone knew what a gentle wife I was. I made his coffee every evening and one evening, when we were alone together, I put a little of the poison in his cup . . .'

Alix paused, and carefully rethreaded her needle. She had never acted in her life, but at this moment she was as good as the greatest actress in the world. She was actually living the part of a pitiless poisoner.

'It was very peaceful. I sat watching him. Once he coughed a little and said that he wanted air. I opened the window. Then he said that he could not move from his chair. *In the end he died.*'

She stopped, smiling. It was a quarter to nine. Surely they would come soon.

'How much,' said Gerald, 'did he insure his life for?'

'About two thousand pounds. I used it unwisely and lost it. I went back to my office work, but I never meant to stay there long. Then I met another man. He didn't know that I'd been married before. He was a younger man, quite good-looking, and he had quite a bit of money. We were married quietly in Sussex. He didn't want to insure his life, but of course his money would come to me if he died. He liked me to make his coffee just as my first husband had done.'

Alix smiled thoughtfully, and added simply, 'I make very good coffee.'

Then she went on: 'I had several friends in the village where we were living. They were very sorry for me when my husband died suddenly of heart failure one evening after dinner. I didn't really like the doctor. I don't think that he suspected me, but he was certainly very surprised at my husband's sudden death. This time I received about four thousand pounds, and this time I saved it. Then, you see—'

But she was interrupted. Gerald Martin was pointing at her with one shaking hand, and holding his throat with the other.

'The coffee — it was the coffee!'

She looked at him in surprise.

'I understand now why it was bitter. You devil! You've poisoned me.'

His hands seized the arms of the chair. He was ready to jump on her. Alix moved away from him to stand by the fireplace. She was thoroughly frightened again. She opened her lips to tell him the truth — and then paused. In another minute he would attack her. She looked at him steadily and with authority.

'Yes,' she said, 'I've poisoned you. Already the poison is working. At this moment you can't move from your chair — you can't move . . .'

If she could keep him there — even for a few minutes.

Ah! What was that? She heard footsteps on the road. She heard the noise of the garden gate. Then footsteps on the path outside, and the outer door opening.

'*You can't move,*' she said again.

Then she slipped past him and rushed from the room to fall, fainting, into Dick Windyford's arms.

'Good heavens! Alix!' he cried.

Then he turned to the man with him, a tall strong policeman.

'Go and see what's been happening in that room!'

He laid Alix down carefully in a chair and bent over her.

'My little girl,' he said softly. 'My poor little girl. What have they been doing to you?'

Her eyelids moved once, and her lips just whispered his name. The policeman returned and touched Dick on the arm. 'There's nothing in that room, sir, except a man sitting in a chair. It looks as if he'd had some kind of bad shock, and . . .'

'Yes?'

'Well, sir, he's – dead.'

They were surprised suddenly to hear Alix's voice.

'*And in the end*,' she said, as if she was in a dream, '*he died.*'

An Unpleasant Man   *Cyril Hare*

The police car, which had been called from the main police station at Markhampton, drove quickly around the edge of the American airfield and on up the village street. It was half past eight on a fine spring morning, and the road was empty except for a line of the American army cars that now seemed to be a common sight on the country roads of that particular part of England. Sergeant Place of the Markshire Police, who was sitting beside the young driver, looked at them with little pleasure. It was not that he had any real objection to Americans. On the whole, they did not behave worse than the local people. But when they did behave badly, the way in which they did so was different. This was, in itself, an offence to Place, who had been brought up to believe in the regular order of things. Consider this business at Hawthorn House, for example – there was sure to be an American mixed up in it, and that would cause trouble.

Hawthorn House was an old, rather dark little house which stood by itself on the far side of the village. There were many like it in the area. The owners rented them out to visiting army officers, and profited greatly by asking high rents. As the police car reached the entrance, the police doctor's car came up behind it, and the three men went into the house together.

Sergeant Place was rather relieved when the door was opened by someone who was clearly an Englishman – a middle-aged man with rather unhealthy skin, wearing the dull clothes of a manservant.

'Will you come this way, please?' he said in the accepted language of his profession, and led them upstairs to the best bedroom. He opened the door and stood to one side for them to enter.

The man in the bed had certainly been dead for some hours, because the body was already cold. Sergeant Place judged that he was about forty-five. There was little character in the round face. He was dressed for bed in expensive and rather bright clothes, which did not seem to go with the simple furniture. On the table by the bed there was a half-empty bottle, an empty glass, and a small round medicine box which was also empty. On the floor beside the table was a letter with an envelope that was simply addressed to 'Mr William Harris'. It had not come by post. Place gave some instructions to the young police driver and left the room. He found the servant standing in the passage just outside the door.

'Let's go downstairs, shall we?' he suggested. 'We can talk better there.'

The man went before him down the narrow staircase into the sitting room. Place watched him closely as he stood, respectful but anxious, in front of the empty fireplace.

'You haven't been here long have you?' he began.

'I – no sir, only three days. We were in London before that. But how–?'

'Easy,' said Place with a smile. 'You forgot to lower your head for the wooden beam at the top of the stairs. This place was let with furniture, I suppose. To an American?'

'No sir, not to an American. Mr Harris is – was – English. But I understood that he had lived in the United States for some years and, I may say, picked up some American habits.'

He was talking more easily now. Place's smile usually made people feel comfortable.

'And what's your name?'

'Wilson, sir. Thomas Wilson.'

'Well, Wilson, tell me when you found out that your master was dead.'

'When I went in this morning to give him his cup of tea, sir.

I didn't touch anything, but rang up the police immediately. I hope that I did right.'

'Quite right. And when had you last seen him before that?'

'Last night, sir, at about 10.30. He'd given me a free evening, and when I came in he was just getting into bed.'

'And what can you tell me about Mr Harris?'

'I can tell you very little, sir. I had only been with him for two weeks. He hired me through Chiltern's, the employment agency. No doubt you've heard of it, sir. But I can tell you that his ways were – well, a little strange, sir.'

'Strange? Well, naturally. You've just told me that he had American habits.'

'No, sir, I don't mean that they were strange in that way. He was afraid.'

'What of?'

'Oh – of people, sir. And of Americans, especially. That was why he took this house. He said that there were too many Americans in London, and that he wanted to get right away from them.'

Sergeant Place laughed at the idea of a person coming to Markshire in order to get away from that particular danger.

'He chose the wrong area to come to, then,' he said. 'Didn't he know that the Americans had an army base in the village?'

'It seems that he didn't, sir. I think that it was a great shock to him when he found out. Only yesterday he said to me—'

Place thought to himself that by helping these anxious witnesses to get over their fear, you encouraged them to wander on for ever. He decided that he had better return to the more important matter of Mr Harris's death. He interrupted Wilson.

'Do you know anything about this?' he said, and produced the envelope which he had taken from the bedroom.

'That, sir? Oh yes, I gave it to Mr Harris last night when I came in.'

45

'Where did it come from?'

'The staff officer gave it to me to give him.'

'I don't understand. What staff officer?'

'I was going to tell you, sir, when you interrupted me,' the man said patiently. 'It happened yesterday morning. Mr Harris and I drove down to the village to do some shopping and we had to stop in the village street where they are repairing the road. They were only letting through one line of cars at a time. There was an American army car coming the other way. This staff officer was in the front, and as he passed he seemed to recognize Mr Harris, sir.'

'How did you know that?'

'He spoke to him, sir. Just one word. It sounded like "Blimey!"'*

'Not a very American word, Wilson. Are you sure it wasn't "Limey"?'

'It could have been that, sir. What does that mean, if I may ask?'

'It's a rather insulting name for an Englishman. Go on.'

'Whatever it was, it seemed to trouble Mr Harris a good deal, sir. He drove on as soon as the car had passed, and never stopped in the village at all. We did our shopping in Markhampton. Then last night I saw the staff officer again.'

'Where?'

'At the local inn, sir – the Spotted Dog. I was spending my evening there. The place was full of American soldiers, and he was with them. He recognized me immediately and spoke to me. He bought me one or two drinks and then he – well, he began to ask me questions, sir.'

'He found out who you were and where you were living and so on?'

'Exactly, sir. Then, just before the inn closed, he asked the innkeeper for a bit of paper and an envelope and wrote

* blimey: a word used to express surprise.

46

something and told me to give it to Mr Harris. So I did, sir.'

'And you don't know what was written in the letter?'

'Naturally not, sir.' In spite of his polite voice, the man was offended. Sergeant Place recognized this and smiled slightly.

'You might be interested to know. Here it is.' Place read: 'Well, Limey, this is quite a surprise. I'll pay a visit to your little hiding place about midday tomorrow, so you had better be there.'

'Is that all, sir?'

'That's all. And it's signed – Joe.'

'That's the name of the staff officer, no doubt, sir.

'If you saw him again, would you recognize him?'

'All these Americans look very much alike to me, sir, but I expect I would.'

'Well,' said Place as he put the letter away, 'that appears to be all. You gave him that letter, and he's dead. He died of – what exactly did he die of, Doctor?' he asked, as the police doctor came into the room.

'A form of poison, without doubt. I can't say more until we've made a thorough examination. He died about eight to ten hours ago, I should think. I can see no sign of violence. I am going now unless you still want me. Shall I make arrangements to have the body moved?'

'Not just yet, thank you, doctor. I would prefer not to have anyone in the house until the afternoon. We may have a visitor about midday.'

When the doctor had gone, Place called to the young driver, who was upstairs.

'Percy?'

'Yes, Sergeant Place?'

'Take the car round to the back of the house, will you? I don't want it to be seen from the road.'

Percy came downstairs.

'I've searched his room fairly thoroughly,' he remarked. 'He's

47

got some very bright American clothes. I found this in a drawer – I thought that it might interest you.'

He handed to Place a small pile of newspaper cuttings, and went out to the car. Place saw that they were all taken from American papers and were arranged so that the most recent was on top. It was the top one, in fact, that caught his eye. 'This morning John Benjamin Spencer was put to death for the murder of bank guard Edward Hart,' it began. He looked through the rest of the cuttings and found a familiar name. 'William S. Harris, who was born in England and was a former business partner of the defendant, was today called as a witness in the case against John B. Spencer.'

'Do you need me any more, sir?' said Wilson, who was still in the room.

'No,' said Place, whose attention was fixed on the newspaper cuttings. 'Yes,' he added immediately. 'What did Mr Harris do when you gave him the note?'

'He read it, sir.'

'Anything else?'

'Then he sent me downstairs to get a bottle of alcohol and two glasses.'

'Two glasses?'

'Mr Harris was very informal,' the man explained. 'He had American habits, although he was an Englishman like you or me. He asked me to have a drink with him. He was not at all like any other gentleman that I have served.'

Place looked at his unhealthy face and his unsteady fingers, which were yellow with tobacco. 'You drink quite a lot, don't you, Wilson?' he said.

'A little, sir, I must admit – now and again.'

'Is that why you lost your last post?'

'No sir!' He was deeply offended. 'I've been in first-class service all my life and my employers have always been pleased with me. My last position was with Lord Gaveston. I was in his service for five years, and I only lost that post when he and his wife separated and the family broke up. This position was not really good enough for me. I accepted it because Chiltern's agency had nothing else to offer at the time, and the wages were good. Chiltern's know me, sir, and they would put me forward for the best employment. Ask them now, if you don't believe me. The telephone number is Belgrave 8290. You can make a long-distance telephone call immediately, if you like.'

'I think you've said enough, Wilson. There's no need to get excited,' said Place, to calm him down.

'I'm sorry, sir, but a man in my position depends on having a good name. I've had a shock and – and I've had no breakfast this morning yet.'

'Just finish your story. You said that you brought Mr Harris the bottle of alcohol . . .'

'That's right, sir. When I brought it, he was sitting on the side of his bed. He poured some of it out into two glasses, and we both had one. Then he told me to leave the bottle and his glass with him and we said good night. I didn't see him again until I found him this morning.'

'Thank you, Wilson; you've been most helpful. Now go to the kitchen and get yourself something to eat.'

Place looked at his watch. It was just nine o'clock. He had a three-hour wait, if Staff Officer Joe came on time . . . if he chose to come at all. If he did not, it would not be easy to find him. He considered how many staff officers at the big American base were called Joe. The situation could have been worse, of course. The name on the letter might have been Butch or Red. Half the men in the American forces seemed to share those strange names. But Joe was nearly as common. For now, he must wait.

A policeman often has to wait, but this time Place found it quite pleasant. He had a comfortable chair to wait in and a pile of newspaper cuttings to read. The cuttings reported a very ordinary kind of murder – a guard had been killed during a bank robbery. And, like many murderers, John B. Spencer looked a very ordinary young man in his photographs. As for Mr Harris, it seemed that he had been lucky only to have been a witness and not to have been charged with Spencer. Or had he been so lucky? Sergeant Place was not so sure when he thought of the man who had been frightened and was now lying upstairs. He read the cuttings again and again until he heard Percy call from the hall, 'Here he comes, Sergeant Place!'

Place opened the door for a young man in army uniform, who looked at him in surprise.

'Have I come to the right place?' he asked. 'They told me that this was Mr Harris's house.'

'They told you quite correctly. Come in.'

The visitor entered. He looked hard at Place, and then at Percy.

'You're policemen, aren't you?' he said. 'What's happened?'

'Did you write a letter to Mr Harris last night?'

'I did.'

'He was found dead in bed this morning.'

The young man took a little time to think this information over. His face showed no expression. As Place watched him, he thought that the line of his jaw seemed familiar.

'Well . . .' he said at last, 'that saves a lot of trouble, doesn't it?'

'Does it?' Place asked. 'That rather depends on why you wanted to see Mr Harris.'

'Perhaps we needn't discuss that at present. I'm grateful that you gentlemen gave me the news, that's all. I'd better go now.'

'Wait a minute. Before you go, there are two questions that I'd like to ask you. What sort of man was the late Mr Harris?'

'He was an extremely unpleasant man,' said the staff officer. 'What's the other question?'

'Is your name Spencer, by any chance?'

'Yes, I'm Joseph Wilbur Spencer.'

'And John Benjamin Spencer?'

'He was my brother.'

'Thank you, Spencer. You have told me all I want to know. Now would you care to see the body and make sure that it is Mr Harris?'

'Sir,' said Spencer, 'during my stay in this country I have developed a great respect for your police – a very great respect. If you tell me that Harris is dead, I don't ask for any proof. No sir! The word of the British police is good enough for me. But I will say this: you've given me a piece of news that is going to make the people in my home town very thankful when it is known, as certainly it will be. And now I will say good day to you.'

'Percy, ask Wilson to come in here for a minute,' said Place, after the visitor had gone.

Percy went out to the kitchen, and returned with a smile on his face.

'I think that Wilson decided against breakfast and had a few drinks instead,' he said. 'I can't wake him up.'

'Well – he's had a shock, as he said himself. I don't really need him. We'll ask Scotland Yard to send a man round to Chiltern's. Perhaps they can tell us something about the late Mr Harris. We shall have to find out more than the fact that he was unpleasant.'

He picked up the telephone.

'I want to make a trunk call, please, miss. Get me—'

He put the instrument down with a crash.

'Percy?' he shouted. 'Get the car out, quick, and go after that staff officer. Bring him back immediately – by force, if necessary.'

To a confused and rather annoyed Spencer, Sergeant Place said, 'I'm sorry, but I must know for certain if the body upstairs is really Harris.'

'If you say so, sir. I've no real objection to dead bodies, but I would have thought—'

He stopped suddenly as Place threw open the door to the kitchen.

'Limey!' he cried. He bent over the half-conscious figure, which was breathing heavily. 'They said that you were dead!'

'Not yet,' said Place cheerfully. 'But he soon will be. There is less delay over British criminal cases than over yours, I expect. Now, if you don't mind, we'll go upstairs and examine the body of Thomas Wilson – the poor, harmless servant whom Harris poisoned last night when he got your note. He hoped that when you spread the news of his death, he wouldn't be troubled by John Spencer's friends and relatives again. It was a neat plan, and it might have succeeded, if he hadn't forgotten that he was playing the part of an English servant and talked about long-distance telephone calls instead of trunk calls. As he told me himself, he'd picked up a lot of American habits while he was away. I expect that he came down here specially in order to be seen by you and then to pretend to kill himself. Mr Harris was quite a clever criminal.'

'Didn't I say that he was an unpleasant man?' said Staff Officer Spencer.

The Unlucky Theatre   *Elliott O'Donnell*

For many years there was a theatre in London which was regarded as unlucky because for a very long time no play produced in it was a success. It was called the Mohawk and it had changed its name many times, but none of the names brought it any good luck. Also, people believed that it was visited by ghosts, and this gave it an even worse name.

When my friend Fernaghan heard about this theatre, he was eager to spend a night there. He came from an old Irish family which had, for many centuries, taken an interest in the ways and habits of ghosts.

He asked me if I knew who owned the theatre, and I told him that I believed the owner was Peter Lindsey. Fernaghan soon went to see him and asked if he could keep watch in the theatre for a night. Lindsey agreed on condition that he did not tell the newspapers, and that whatever happened was kept a secret. It was arranged that Fernaghan would go to the stage door at eleven o'clock on a Monday night in June, and that he would be admitted when he rang three times.

Fernaghan was looking forward eagerly to the night, and at last it arrived. He went to the Mohawk at the correct hour, rang the stage-door bell three times, and was let in by the night watchman, John Ward. On this particular occasion Ward was allowed to go home since Fernaghan was taking his place. Ward showed him round the building, explained to him what to do if there was a fire, and left him alone in the theatre. The place seemed lonely, and after Ward had gone there was an uncomfortable stillness; this was broken only by occasional noises such as one hears in old, empty buildings at night. Fernaghan had never imagined that a theatre could be so quiet.

He wandered up and down stairs and along the passages on various floors, looked at the seating areas and then went round behind the stage. The dust lay thick on the boards, and there were signs everywhere of lack of care and attention.

Fernaghan was looking at the remains of a large black insect, and hoping that there were no more live ones around, when he heard a movement in the nearest dressing room. He slowly opened the dressing-room door and looked in. A man was doing something to a stage sword. The man turned round and saw Fernaghan. A guilty, surprised look appeared in his eyes and, since Ward had told him that there was nobody in the building, Fernaghan asked him what he was doing there. There was something strange about the man. His clothes had long been out of fashion and somehow he did not seem quite real.

'Who are you,' Fernaghan asked, 'and what are you doing to that sword?'

He took a step towards the man, who suddenly and without explanation melted away. This gave Fernaghan a shock, but he gradually calmed himself, and although he was still rather shaken, he continued to wander round the dusty old place.

When it was nearly one o'clock by his watch, he thought that it was time to have something to eat. So he sat below the stage, eating some cold chicken and drinking some hot coffee. While he was drinking, he had the feeling that someone was watching him. He looked around him and got such a shock that he almost dropped his cup.

At the edge of the stage was a tall, graceful woman with dark hair and eyes. She was beautiful, but the paleness of her face was striking and very ghostly. She was looking anxiously around the theatre, and when she seemed satisfied that there was no cause for anxiety, she slipped silently across the stage and out of sight.

Fernaghan thought that he had had enough shocks and that he had better leave the Mohawk, because he certainly did not want to see a third ghost. But as he did not like to give up on anything, he stayed on.

He looked slowly round the theatre. How lonely it seemed! What a feeling of sadness and emptiness surrounded it! There was no sign of life anywhere. He thought of the many feet that had stepped out on the stage, of the attractive faces whose beautiful eyes and smiles had given pleasure to so many people. Where were those well-known actors and actresses now? Probably they were all dead and forgotten.

He leaned back in his seat, closed his eyes and dreamed of the past. Suddenly he heard voices. He opened his eyes, and to his surprise he was no longer alone. The seats were completely filled with people dressed in a style of long ago. The house was full but, like the man in the dressing room, these people did not seem real. Their faces were as pale as those of the dead and there was something unpleasantly inhuman about them.

The woman whom Fernaghan had seen on the edge of the stage was now seated alone in one of the more expensive seats, in a box. She wore a rich evening dress of the kind that might have been fashionable in the early years of the nineteenth century. She was leaning forward and watching the stage with great attention.

The musicians below the stage were playing an old tune which had once, no doubt, been popular, but which had since been forgotten. They stopped suddenly as the curtain rose. The scene was a wood, in which two men were about to have a sword fight. One man was tall with fair hair and a beard; the other was dark. At a signal they began to fight.

There was an immediate silence in the theatre, which was broken only by the sharp noises of the fight. Fernaghan looked up at the lady in the box, whose beauty held his attention. She was watching every sword stroke of the fighters with the greatest anxiety and excitement.

Suddenly the fair man's sword flashed forward and struck the dark man in the chest. He gave a long cry, took a few unsteady steps and fell. There was a terrible cry from a girl who had been watching from behind a stage tree, and a joyful shout from the lady in the box.

The curtain dropped. In a few moments it rose again, and Fernaghan was shocked to see a row of skeletons in the clothes that they had probably worn in the play. The musicians and the people watching were all skeletons, and as their bony hands showed their approval, the actors smiled and then threw back their heads and burst into devilish laughter. The curtain fell, and the theatre was once again in darkness.

Fernaghan could not bear any more. He hurried out to the street.

Peter Lindsey listened to Fernaghan's account of his ghostly experiences in the Mohawk with great interest, and told him that they might have been the result of an unfortunate event in the theatre in 1803.

A play called *The Watching Eyes* was being performed at the Cascade, as the Mohawk was then named. Two leading actors were in it, Guy Lang and Raymond Ross. Ross was known to be very much in love with Mrs Lang. She encouraged him and repeatedly told him that she hated her husband, who treated her badly.

In the play there was a fight between Lang and Ross, and one night Ross killed Lang. The stage swords always had rubber buttons on their points so that no one would be hurt, but on this occasion the sword used by Ross had no button. It was always thought that Mrs Lang was responsible and that she intended her lover, Ross, to kill Lang. It was never known for certain whether Ross knew about her intentions, and since his guilt could not be proved, he simply lost his job.

Mrs Lang married a man called Lord Delahoo, whom she had known for some time. Because of the suspicion of murder that was connected with it, the theatre was closed down, and when it opened again it was no longer called the Cascade.

'From that time on,' Lindsey said, 'people have claimed that there are ghosts in the theatre and no play produced in it has ever been a success. It has cost me a lot of money and worry, and if I can't sell it I'll have it pulled down.'

But it was so well known for its ghosts and the bad luck it brought that he could not sell it, so he had it pulled down and sold the land on which it had stood.

The Mezzotint   *M. R. James*

Mr Williams, whose job involved adding to his university's collection of prints and drawings, was a regular customer of the well-known London art dealer, J. W. Britnell. Mr Britnell would send out excellent lists of his large and ever-changing collection, which included plans and old drawings of country houses, churches and towns in England and Wales. These lists were, of course, very important to Mr Williams, but he bought regularly rather than in great quantity; he expected Mr Britnell to fill the less important holes in the university collection rather than to supply him with rare works.

Then in February of last year a list from Mr Britnell appeared on Mr Williams's desk, and with it a letter from the dealer himself. This letter read as follows:

Dear Sir,

We beg to call your attention to Number 978 in our enclosed list, which we shall be glad to send for your examination.

Yours,

J. W. BRITNELL .

When Mr Williams turned to Number 978, he found the following entry:

978   *Unknown.* Interesting mezzotint: view of a country house, early part of the last century. 15 by 10 inches; black frame £2 2 shillings

It was not specially exciting, and the price seemed high. But as Mr Britnell, who knew his business and his customer, seemed to think well of it, Mr Williams wrote a postcard asking for the picture to be sent on approval, together with some other prints and drawings which appeared in the same list. And so he moved on, without much excitement, to the ordinary work of the day.

A package of any kind always arrives a day later than you expect it and the one from Mr Britnell was no exception. It was delivered to Mr Williams's office by the Saturday afternoon post, but after he had left the office. A servant, therefore, brought it round to his rooms in college so that he would not have to wait until Monday for an opportunity to examine what was inside and return what he did not wish to keep. And that's where he found it when he came in to tea with a friend.

The only object with which I am concerned was the rather large, black-framed mezzotint that was described in Mr Britnell's list. It was not of a high quality, and a mezzotint which is not of a high quality is, perhaps, the worst sort of print there is. It showed a view of the front of a not very large eighteenth-century country house. The house had three rows of plain windows and some interesting features. There were trees on either side, and in front there was a large area of well-cut grass. The words 'A. W. F. *sculpsit*'* were written along the narrow edge of the picture, but no other words appeared on it. The whole thing gave one the feeling that it was the work of someone with little experience, and Mr Williams could not imagine why Mr Britnell was demanding two pounds and two shillings for such an object. He turned it over with a good deal of amusement. On the back was a piece of paper, the left-hand half of which had been torn off. Only the ends of two lines of writing remained: the first had the letters '–ngley Hall'; the second, '–ssex'.

Mr Williams thought that it would, perhaps, be just worth the trouble of finding out where the place was, and this he could do

* sculpsit: a Latin word. Here it means 'made (this picture)'.

easily with the help of a map. He would then return the picture to Mr Britnell with some sharp remarks about that gentleman's judgment.

When the lamps were lit, because it was now dark, and the tea was made, the friend − let us call him Dr Binks − took up the framed print and said: 'What's this place, Williams?'

'That's just what I'm going to try to find out,' said Williams, as he went to the shelf for a map. 'Look at the back. Somethingley Hall, in either Sussex or Essex. Half the name has gone, you see. You don't happen to know it, I suppose?'

'It's from that man Britnell, I suppose, isn't it?' said Binks. 'Is it for our collection?'

'Well, I think that I would buy it if the price was five shillings,' said Williams; 'but for some strange reason he wants over two pounds for it. I can't imagine why. It's not a good print and there aren't even any figures to give it life.'

'I certainly don't think it's worth as much as that,' said Binks; 'but I don't think it's so badly done. The moonlight seems rather good to me; and it looks to me as if there are figures, or at least a figure, just on the edge in front.'

'Let's look,' said Williams. 'Well, it's true that the sense of light is rather cleverly done. Where's your figure? Oh, yes! Just the head, right in the front of the picture.'

And it was true, although it was little more than a black spot on the extreme edge of the print, that there was the head of a man or a woman. It was well wrapped up, its back was turned and it was looking towards the house.

Williams had not noticed it before.

'But even so,' he said, 'though it's more skilfully done than I thought at first, I can't spend over two pounds of the university's money on a picture of a place I don't know.'

Doctor Binks, who had work to do, soon went, and Williams spent the remaining time before dinner attempting, without success, to find out the name of the Hall in the picture. 'If the vowel before the 'ng' had been left, there would have been no difficulty,' he thought; 'but as it is, the name may be anything from Guestingley to Langley. There are many more names that end in '–ngley' than I thought; and this useless book doesn't provide a list of endings.'

Dinner in Mr Williams's college was at seven o'clock, but we do not need to know what happened during the meal. Later in the evening, he returned with some friends to his rooms where, doubtless, they played cards and smoked tobacco. After some time, Williams picked up the mezzotint from the table. He did not look at it, but handed it to a person interested in art, and told him where it had come from and the other details which we already know.

The gentleman took it without great excitement, looked at it and then said, in a voice of some interest: 'It's really a very good piece of work, Williams; it has quite an imaginative quality. The light is excellently controlled, it seems to me, and the figure, though it's rather shocking, is somehow very impressive.'

'Yes, isn't it?' said Williams, who was just then pouring out drinks for his other friends and was unable to come across the room to look at the view again.

It was by this time rather late in the evening, and the visitors were beginning to leave. After they had gone, Williams had to write one or two letters and finish some pieces of work. At last, a short time after midnight, he was ready to go to bed, and he lit a small lamp to take to his bedroom. The picture lay face upwards on the table where the last man who had looked at it had put it, and Williams caught sight of it as he put out the sitting-room lamp. He says now, in fact, that if he had been left in the dark at that moment he might have fainted with fear. But, as that did not happen, he was able to steady himself and take a good look at the picture. It was certain – quite impossible, no doubt, but completely certain. In the middle of the grass in front of the unknown house there was a figure where no figure had been at five o'clock that afternoon. It was moving on its hands and knees towards the house, and it was wrapped in strange, black clothing with a white cross on the back.

I do not know what is the right thing to do in a situation of this kind. I can only tell you what Mr Williams did. He took the picture by one corner and carried it across the passage to a second set of rooms which he possessed. There he locked it up in a drawer, locked the doors of both sets of rooms, and went to bed; but first he wrote out and signed an account of the strange change that had taken place in the picture since it had come into his possession.

Sleep came to him rather late, but he was comforted to know that he was not the only witness of the behaviour of the picture. Clearly, the man who had looked at the mezzotint earlier that night had seen the same sort of thing that he himself had seen. If not, he might have started to believe that something seriously wrong was happening either to his eyes or to his mind. As this was fortunately impossible, there were two things he must do in the morning. He must ask a second person to act as a witness and examine the picture with him, and he must make a determined effort to find out the name of the house that was represented in it. He would therefore invite his neighbour, Nisbet, to have breakfast with him, and then he would study a map for the rest of the morning.

Nisbet was free, and arrived at about 9.30. I am sorry to say that his host was not quite dressed, even at this late hour. During breakfast, Williams said nothing about the mezzotint, except that he had a picture about which he wished to have Nisbet's opinion. Those who are familiar with university life can easily imagine the pleasant conversation of two members of Canterbury College during a Sunday morning breakfast. I am

62

forced to say, though, that Williams found it difficult to pay attention. His interest was naturally centred on that very strange picture which was now lying, face downwards, in the drawer in the room opposite.

At last breakfast was finished, and he was able to light his pipe. The moment had arrived for which he had been waiting. His excitement was so great that he was almost trembling. He ran across and unlocked the drawer, then took out the picture – still face downwards – ran back, and put it into Nisbet's hands.

'Now,' he said, 'Nisbet, I want you to tell me exactly what you see in that picture. Describe it in detail, if you don't mind. I'll tell you why in a moment.'

'Well,' said Nisbet, 'I have here a view of a country house – English, I believe – by moonlight.'

'Moonlight? Are you sure of that?'

'Certainly. It seems to be past the full moon, if you wish for details, and there are clouds in the sky.'

'All right. Go on. I'll swear,' added Williams to himself, 'that there was no moon when I saw it first.'

'Well, there isn't much more to be said,' Nisbet continued. 'The house has one – two – three rows of windows, and there are five windows in each row except at the bottom where there's a door instead of the middle one and–'

'But what about figures?' said Williams with marked interest.

'There aren't any,' said Nisbet; 'but–'

'What! There is no figure on the grass in front?'

'Not a thing.'

'You'll swear to that?'

'Certainly. But there's just one other thing.'

'What?'

'Well, one of the windows on the ground floor – to the left of the door – is open.'

'Is it really? Good heavens! He must have got in,' said Williams with great excitement. He hurried to the back of the chair on which Nisbet was sitting and seized the picture from him to check it for himself.

It was quite true. There was no figure, and there was an open window. For a moment Williams was so surprised that he could not speak. Then he went to the writing table and wrote hurriedly for a short time. When he had finished he brought two papers to Nisbet. He asked him to sign the first one, which was the description of the picture that you have just read. And he asked him to read the second one, which was the description that Williams had written the night before.

'What does it all mean?' said Nisbet.

'Exactly,' said Williams. 'Well, there is one thing that I must do – or rather there are three things. First, I must find out what Garwood, who looked at the picture last night, saw. Secondly, I must photograph the thing before it changes further. And thirdly, I must find out where the house is.'

'I can photograph it myself,' said Nisbet, 'and I will. But, you know, I feel as if we were watching some terrible event taking place somewhere. The question is, has it happened already, or is it about to happen? You must find out where the house is.' He looked at the picture again. 'Yes,' he said, 'I expect that you're right: he has got in. And I feel sure that something unpleasant is going to happen in one of the rooms upstairs.'

'I've got an idea,' said Williams. 'I'll take the picture across to old Green.' (Green was the oldest member of the college, and had managed its business for many years.) 'He'll probably know where the house is. The college has property in Essex and Sussex, and he must have travelled a great deal in those parts of England.'

'Yes, he probably will know where it is,' said Nisbet; 'but just let me take my photograph first. Listen, though, I don't think that Green is here today. He wasn't at dinner last night, and I think I heard him say that he would be away on Sunday.'

'Yes, that's true,' said Williams. 'I know that he's gone to Brighton. Well, if you'll take the photograph now, I'll go across to Garwood and get his statement. While I'm doing that, you must keep an eye on it. I'm beginning to think that two pounds and two shillings is not such a high price for it after all.'

In a short time he had returned and brought Mr Garwood with him. Garwood said that when he had seen the figure it was no longer at the edge of the picture, but that it was not far across the grass. He remembered that the figure had had a white mark on the back of its clothing, but he was not sure if it had been a cross. All this was written down and signed, and Nisbet then photographed the picture.

'Now what do you mean to do?' he said. 'Are you going to sit and watch it all day?'

'Well no, I don't think so,' said Williams. 'I rather imagine that we are intended to see the whole thing. You see, between the time that I saw it last night and this morning, there was time for lots of things to happen, but the figure only got into the house. In that time, it could have done its business easily and left again. But as the window is open, I think that it must be inside now. So I feel confident that we can leave it. And, besides, I have an idea that the picture won't change much, if at all, in the daytime. We could go for a walk this afternoon and come in to tea when it gets dark. I shall leave it out on the table here, and lock the door. Then only my servant can get in.'

The three men agreed that this would be a good plan; and so we may leave them alone until five o'clock.

At or near that hour the three returned to Williams's rooms. They were slightly annoyed to see that the door of his rooms was unlocked until they remembered that on Sunday the college servants came for their orders earlier than on weekdays. But a surprise was waiting for them. First, they saw that the picture was leaning against a pile of books on the table, as it had been left. The next thing that they saw was Williams's servant, Robert, who was sitting on a chair opposite it and looking at it with fear in his eyes. Why was this? Robert was known for his excellent manners. He would never normally sit down on his master's chair or appear to take any particular interest in his master's furniture or pictures. In fact he jumped up quickly when the three men entered the room and said: 'I beg your pardon, sir. I shouldn't have sat down.'

'It doesn't matter, Robert,' answered Mr Williams. 'I was meaning to ask you for your opinion of that picture.'

'Well, sir, I know my opinion is worth little in comparison with yours, but I wouldn't hang that picture where my little girl could see it.'

'Wouldn't you, Robert? Why not?'

'No, sir. Well, I remember that once the poor child saw a book with pictures in it that were not nearly so bad as that one there, and we had to sit up with her for three or four nights after that. And if she saw this skeleton, or whatever it is, carrying off the poor baby, she would be in a terrible state. You know what children are like. But what I say is that it doesn't seem the kind of picture to leave about, sir. If anybody saw it accidentally, he might have an unpleasant shock. Do you want anything else this evening, sir? Thank you, sir.'

With these words the excellent man left to visit the rest of his masters. The three gentlemen immediately moved closer to the mezzotint. There was the house, as before, under the clouds and the moon that was no longer full. The window that had been open was shut, and the figure was once more on the grass. But this time it was not moving slowly on hands and knees. Now it stood up straight and was marching quickly, with long steps, towards the front of the picture. The moon was behind it, and the black clothing hung down over its face so that hardly anything of it could be seen. In fact, the little of it that could be seen made the three gentlemen deeply thankful that they could see no more than the white forehead and a few untidy hairs. The head was bent down, and the arms were tightly closed over an object which could just be seen and recognized as a child. It was not possible to say whether it was dead or living. Only the legs of the figure carrying it could be seen clearly, and they were terribly thin.

Between five and seven o'clock the three companions sat and watched the picture in turn. But it never changed. They agreed at last that it would be safe to leave it, and that they would return after dinner and wait for further developments.

They met again as soon as possible. The print was there, but the figure had gone, and the house was quiet in the moonlight. All they could do now was to spend the evening searching through the maps and guidebooks until they found out where the house was. Williams was the lucky person in the end, and perhaps he deserved to be. At 11.30 p.m. he read the following lines from Murray's *Guide to Essex*:

$16\frac{1}{2}$ miles, *Anningley*. The church was originally an interesting building from the twelfth century, but was greatly changed in the last century. It contains the graves of the Francis family whose country house, Anningley Hall, stands just beyond the churchyard in a large park. The family has now died out. The last son disappeared mysteriously in childhood in the year 1802. The father, Mr Arthur Francis, was known in the area as quite a good artist in mezzotint. After his son's disappearance, he lived completely alone at the Hall. He was found dead exactly three years later in the room where he had just completed a mezzotint of the house, copies of which are extremely rare.

This seemed to be the end of the search, and when Mr Green returned to the college he immediately recognized the house as Anningley Hall.

'Is there any kind of explanation of the figure, Green?' Williams asked him.

'I really don't know, Williams. I knew Anningley before I came to this university and there used to be one or two stories about Arthur Francis. He was always very severe with any man whom he suspected of hunting on his land. Gradually he got rid of all such thieves with the exception of one man, called Gawdy, I believe, who continued to take animals from the Hall grounds. Gawdy was the last member of a very old family which, it was said, had once been the most important family in the area. The graves of his relations were inside the church and not out in the churchyard like those of common people, and he felt a good deal of bitterness that his family had lost its former greatness. It was said that Francis could never prove anything against him, but in the end, Francis's keepers caught him in a wood on the edge of the park. I could show you the place even now, because it is right beside some land that used to belong to my uncle. As you can imagine, there was a fight, and this man Gawdy most unluckily shot one of the keepers. Well, that was just what Francis wanted. There was a quick and most unsatisfactory court case, and poor Gawdy was hanged as quickly as possible. I've been shown the place where he was buried. It's on the north side of the church, where they buried any person who had been hanged or who had killed himself. The poor man had no relatives because he was the last member of his family, but people believed that some friend of his must have planned to seize Francis's boy in order to put an end to *his* family, too. But, you know, I should say now that it looks more as if old Gawdy had managed the thing himself. Ugh! I hate to think of it! Have a drink, Williams!'

I have only to add that the picture is now in the Ashleian Collection. It has been tested in order to find out whether the artist used a special kind of ink which could account for its strange behaviour, but without any result. Mr Britnell knew nothing about it except that he was sure that it was an uncommon picture. And although it was carefully watched, it has never been known to change again.

Family Affair   *Margery Allingham*

The newspapers were calling the McGills' house in Chestnut Street 'the *Mary Celeste* house' before Chief Inspector Charles Luke noticed that the two mysteries were alike. He was so shaken that he telephoned Albert Campion and asked him to come over.

They met in the Sun, a quiet little inn in the High Street, and discussed the case in the small public bar which, at that time of day, was empty.

'The two stories *are* alike,' Luke said as he picked up his drink. He was a dark, strong and very active man; and as usual he was talking continuously, using his hands to emphasize his words. 'I'd almost forgotten the *Mary Celeste* mystery, but I read a fresh report of it in the *Morning News* today. Of course, the *Mary Celeste* was a ship, and 29 Chestnut Street is an ordinary, unexciting little house, but in other ways the two stories are nearly the same. There was even a half-eaten breakfast left on the table in both of them. It's very strange, Campion.'

Campion, who was quiet and fair and wore glasses, listened closely as was his habit. And, as usual, he looked a little uncertain of himself; a great many men had failed to take him seriously until it was too late. At the moment he appeared to be slightly amused. He was always entertained by the strength of Luke's excitement.

'You think that you know what has happened to Mr and Mrs McGill, then?' he asked.

'Good heavens, no!' The policeman opened his small, black eyes to their widest. 'I tell you that it's the same story as the mystery of the *Mary Celeste*. They've simply disappeared. One minute they were having breakfast together like every other husband and wife for miles around, and the next minute they

70

had gone without a sign.'

Mr Campion paused. He looked rather self-conscious. 'As I remember the story of the *Mary Celeste*, it was completely unbelievable,' he said at last. 'Consider it: a band of quite ordinary-looking sailors brought a ship called the *Mary Celeste* into Gibraltar, and had a wonderful story to tell. They said that she was found in mid-ocean with all her sails up, but without a single person on board. The details were shocking. There were three cups of tea on the captain's table and they were still warm. In his room there was a box of female clothes which were small enough to be a child's. A cat was asleep in the kitchen, and in a pot on the cooker was a chicken ready to be cooked.' Campion let out a long breath. 'Quite beautiful,' he said, 'but witnesses also swore that although there was no one at the wheel she was still following her course. The court of inquiry found that too much to believe, although they discussed it for as long as they could.'

Luke looked at him sharply.

'That wasn't what the *Morning News* suggested this morning,' he said. 'They called it "the world's favourite unsolved mystery".'

'So it is!' Mr Campion was laughing. 'Because nobody wants an ordinary explanation which uncovers dishonesty. The mystery of the *Mary Celeste* is an excellent example of a story which really is a bit too good to spoil, don't you think?'

'I don't know. I hadn't thought of it.' Luke sounded slightly annoyed. 'I was just telling you the main story of the two events – actually, 1872 is rather too long ago for me. But 29 Chestnut Street is certainly my business, and I'm not allowing any witness to use his imagination in this inquiry. Just give your attention to the facts and details, Campion.'

Luke put down his glass.

'Consider the McGills,' he said. 'They seem ordinary, sensible people. Peter McGill was twenty-eight and his wife Maureen was a year younger. They had been married for three years and got

71

along well together. For the first two years they had to live with his mother, while they were waiting for the right kind of house to become available. But they weren't very happy there, so they rented two rooms from Maureen's married sister. Then after six months this house in Chestnut Street was offered to them.'

'Did they have any money troubles?' Mr Campion asked.

'No.' Luke clearly thought that this was very unusual. 'Peter seems to be the one member of the family who had nothing to complain about. He works in the office of a company that makes locks, and they are very pleased with him. He is known for not spending more than he can afford and, in any case, his salary was raised recently. I saw his employer this morning and he was really anxious, poor old boy. He liked the young man and had nothing but praise for him.'

'What about Mrs McGill?'

'She's another good type. She's steady and careful, and she remained at work until a few months ago when her husband decided that she should leave her job in order to enjoy the new house and raise a family. She certainly did her housework well. The place is still in excellent order although it has been empty for six weeks.'

For the first time Mr Campion's eyes lit up with interest. 'Forgive me,' he said, 'but do the police usually enter a case of missing persons so quickly? What is it that you are looking for, Charles? A body? Or bodies?'

'Not officially,' Luke said. 'But I can't help asking myself what we shall find. We came into the case quickly because we heard about it quickly. The situation was unusual and the family were rather frightened. That's the explanation of that.' He paused for a moment. 'Come along and have a look at the house. We'll come back and have another drink after you've seen it, but this is something that's really special, and I want your help.'

Mr Campion followed him out into the network of neat little

streets which ran between rows of box-shaped houses set in neat little flower gardens.

'We go down to the end and along to the right,' Luke said, as he pointed towards the end of the road. 'I'll tell you the rest of the story as we go. On 12th June, Bertram Heskith, who is the husband of Maureen's older sister and lives in the next-but-one house, dropped in to see them as he usually did about 7.30 in the morning. He came in by the back door, which was open, and found a half-eaten breakfast for two on the table in the bright new kitchen. No one was around, so he sat down to wait.'

Luke's long hands were busily forming the scene in the air as he talked, and Mr Campion felt that he could almost see the little room with its inexpensive but not unattractive furniture and the flowers in the window.

'Bertram is a toy salesman and one of a large family,' Luke went on. 'He's got no work at the moment but he's not unhappy about it. He talks rather a lot, he's grown a little too big for his clothes and he enjoys a drink, but he's got a sharp mind – too sharp, I would say. He would have noticed anything unusual. But in fact the tea in the pot was still warm, so he poured himself a cup, picked up the newspaper which was lying open on the floor by Peter McGill's chair and started to read it. After a time he realized that the house was very quiet, so he went into the hall and shouted up the stairs. As there was no reply he went up and found that the bed was unmade, that the bathroom was still warm and wet with steam, and that Maureen's everyday hat, coat and handbag were lying on a chair. Bertram came down, examined the rest of the house, then went out into the garden. Maureen had been doing some washing before breakfast and the clothes on the line were almost dry. Otherwise, the little square of land was quite empty.' He gave Campion a quick look out of the corner of his eye. 'And that, my boy, is all,' he said. 'Neither Peter nor Maureen has been seen since. As they didn't appear again, Bertram told the rest of the family and, after two days, went to the police.'

'Really?' Campion showed some interest. 'Is that *all* that you know?'

'Not quite, but the rest of the information is hardly helpful.' Luke sounded almost pleased. 'Wherever they are, they're not in the house or garden. If they walked out, no one saw them; and they would need both skill and luck for that, because they were surrounded by concerned relatives and friends. The only things that are definitely missing are two clean sheets. A "fine pair of sheets" one lady called them.'

Mr Campion looked surprised.

'That's a small detail,' he said. 'I suppose that there is no sign of any crime?'

'Crime is really becoming quite common in London. I don't know what's happening to the old place,' Luke said sorrowfully. 'But this house seemed healthy and happy enough. The McGills appear to have been ordinary, pleasant young people, although there are one or two little things that make one think. As far as we can find out, Peter did not catch his usual train to work, but we have one witness – a third cousin of his – who says that she followed him up the street from his house to the corner just as she did every morning during the week. At the top of the street she went in one direction and she thought that he went in the other as usual. But no one else seems to have seen him and she's probably mistaken. Well, now, here we are. Stand here for a minute.'

He had paused on the path of a narrow street, shaded by trees and lined with pairs of pleasant little houses.

'The next house along here belongs to the Heskiths,' he went on, lowering his voice. 'We'll walk rather quickly past it because we don't want any more help from Bertram at the moment. He's a good man but he believes that Maureen's property is in his trust, and the way in which he follows me around makes me feel self-conscious. His house is Number 25, and 29 is next but one. Now Number 31, which is actually joined to 29 on the other side, is locked up; the old lady who owns it is in hospital. In 33 live two sisters who are aunts of Peter's. They moved there soon after him and Maureen.

'One has lost her husband, and the other is unmarried, but they are both very interested in the nephew and his wife. The one whose husband has died speaks quite kindly about her young relatives, but her unmarried sister, Miss Dove, is rather critical of them. She told me that Maureen was careless with money, and I think that from time to time she had had a few words with the girl on the subject. I heard about the "fine pair of sheets" from her. I believe that she had told Maureen she shouldn't have bought something so expensive, but Maureen had saved up a long time for them.'

Luke laughed. 'Women are like that,' he continued. 'They get a desire for something, and they make sure that they have it. Miss Dove says that she watched Maureen hanging out the sheets on the line early in the morning of the day she disappeared. She has an upstairs window in her house from which she can just see part of the garden of 29 – if she stands on a chair.'

He smiled. 'For some reason she was doing that at about half past six on the day the McGills disappeared, and she is quite sure that she saw them hanging on the line – the sheets, I mean. She recognized them by the pattern along the top edge. They're certainly not in the house now. Miss Dove suggests delicately that I should search Bertram's house for them!'

Mr Campion looked thoughtful, though his mouth was smiling.

'It's quite a story,' he said quietly. 'The whole thing just can't have happened. How very strange, Charles. Did anybody else see Maureen that morning? Could she have walked out of the front door and come up the street with the sheets over her arm and not

75

have been noticed? I'm not asking if she *would* have done so, but if she *could*.'

'No,' said Luke. 'Even if she had wanted to do so, which is unlikely, it's almost impossible. There are the cousins opposite, you see. They live over there in the house with the red flowers, directly in front of Number 29. It is one of them who says that she followed Peter up the road that morning. Also there's an old Irish grandmother who sits up in bed in the window of the front room all day. You can't completely trust what she says – for example, she can't remember if Peter came out of the house at his usual time that day – but she would have noticed if Maureen had come out. No one saw Maureen that morning except Miss Dove who, as I told you, watched her hanging the sheets on the line. The newspaper comes early. The milkman heard her washing machine when he left his bottles at the back door, but he did not see her.'

'What about the postman?'

'He can't help. He hasn't been doing this work for very long and can't even remember if he called at Number 29. It's a long street and, as he says, the houses are all alike. He gets to 29 at about 7.25 and doesn't often meet anybody at that hour. He wouldn't recognize the McGills if he saw them, in any case. Come on in, Campion – look around and see what you think.'

Mr Campion followed his friend up a narrow garden path. A police officer stood on guard at the front door. Mr Campion looked back over his shoulder just in time to see a movement behind the curtains in the house opposite. Then a tall, thin woman, whose face was completely expressionless, walked down the path of the next-but-one house and said hello to Luke as she paused at her gate before going back.

'Miss Dove,' said Luke unnecessarily, as he opened the door to Number 29 Chestnut Street.

The house held few surprises for Mr Campion. It was almost

exactly as he had imagined it. There was not very much furniture in the hall and front room, but the kitchen was clearly used a great deal and possessed a character of its own. Someone without much money, but who liked nice things, had lived there. He or she – and he thought that it was probably she – had been generous, too, in spite of her efforts to save, because he noticed little things which had clearly been bought at the door from beggars. The breakfast table had been left exactly as Bertram Heskith had found it, and his cup was still there.

Campion wandered through the house without saying anything, and Luke followed him. The scene was just as he had been told. There was no sign of packing, hurry or violence. There were night clothes on a chair in the bathroom. The woman's coat and handbag were on a chair in the bedroom and contained the usual mixture of things, including two pounds, three shillings and a few pennies, and a set of keys.

Mr Campion looked at everything – the clothes hanging neatly in the cupboards, and even the flowers that had died from lack of water. But the only thing which seemed to interest him was a photograph, taken at Peter and Maureen's marriage, which he found in a silver frame on the dressing table.

Although it was a very ordinary picture, he stood in front of it for a long time in deep thought. As sometimes happens, the two figures in the centre attracted less attention than the rest of the group of guests, who were laughing cheerfully. Maureen, with her graceful figure and big dark eyes, looked gentle and a little frightened, and Peter, although solid and with a determined chin, had an expression of anxiety on his face which compared strangely with Bertram Heskith's confident smile.

'You can see what sort of a person Bertram is,' said Luke. 'You wouldn't call him a gentleman, but he's not a man who imagines things. When he says that he felt the two had been in the house that morning, as safe and happy as usual, I believe him.'

'Miss Dove isn't here?' said Campion, still looking at the group in the photograph.

'No. Her sister is there, though. And that's the girl from the house opposite, who thinks that she saw Peter go up the road.'

Luke pointed to the face of another girl. 'There's another sister here, and the rest are cousins. I understand that the picture doesn't do justice to Maureen's looks. Everybody says that she was a very pretty girl . . .' He corrected himself. 'Is, I mean.'

'Peter looks a reasonable type to me,' said Mr Campion, 'although a little uncomfortable, perhaps.'

'I wonder.' Luke spoke thoughtfully. 'The Heskiths had another photo of him and in that there was a kind of hardness and determination about his face. In the war I knew an officer with a face like that. Generally, he was quite a gentle man, but when something upset him, he behaved very decisively. But that's unimportant. Come and examine the clothesline and then you'll know as much as I do.'

Luke led the way to the back and stood for a moment on the stone path, which ran under the kitchen window and separated the house from the small square of grass which formed the garden.

On the right, the garden was separated from the neighbouring gardens by a fence and a line of bushes. On the left, the plants in the uncared-for garden of the old lady who was in hospital had grown up so high that one was sheltered from the eyes of everyone except Miss Dove. Mr Campion supposed that, at that moment, she was standing on her chair to watch them. At the bottom there were a garden hut and a few fruit trees.

Luke pointed to the empty line which hung above the grass. 'I brought in the washing,' he said. 'The Heskiths were afraid that it would decay, and there seemed no reason to leave it outside.'

'What's in the hut?'

'A spade, a fork and a few other garden tools,' said Luke. 'Come and look. The floor is made of beaten earth and it has clearly not been dug up for years. I suppose that we'll have to dig it up in the end, but it will be a waste of time.'

Mr Campion went over and looked into the wooden hut. It was tidy and dusty, and the floor was dry and hard. Outside, an old ladder leaned against the high brick wall at the end of the garden.

Mr Campion carefully tried the strength of the old ladder. It supported his weight, so he climbed up and looked over the wall. There was a narrow path between the wall and the fence of the back garden of the house in the next street.

'That's an old path that leads down between the two rows of houses,' Luke said. 'This isn't really a very friendly area, you know. The people in Chestnut Street think that they're of a better class than the people in Philpott Road, which is the road on the other side of the path.'

Mr Campion got down from the ladder. He was smiling and his eyes were bright.

'Do you think anybody in Philpott Road noticed her?' he said. 'She must have been carrying the sheets.'

Luke turned round slowly and looked at him in surprise.

'Are you suggesting that she simply walked down the garden and over the wall and out? In the clothes in which she'd been washing? It's crazy. Why would she do it? And did her husband go with her?'

'No, I think that he went down Chestnut Street as usual and turned back down this path as soon as he came to the other end of it near the station. Then he picked up his wife, and went off with her through Philpott Road to catch the bus. They only needed to go as far as Broadway in order to find a taxi.'

Luke was still completely in the dark.

'But *why*?' he demanded. 'Why should they disappear in the middle of breakfast on a Monday morning? And why should they take the sheets? Young married people can do the most unlikely things – but there are limits, Campion! They didn't take their savings books, you know. There isn't much in them but they're still in the writing desk in the front room. What are you suggesting, Campion?'

Campion walked slowly back onto the grass.

'I expect that the sheets were dry and that she'd put them into the clothes basket before breakfast,' he began slowly. 'As she ran out of the house, she saw them lying there and couldn't stop herself from taking them with her. The husband must have been annoyed with her, but people are like that. When they're running away from a fire, they save the strangest things.'

'But she wasn't running away from a fire.'

'Wasn't she!' Mr Campion laughed. 'Listen, Charles. If the postman called, he reached the house at 7.25. I think that he did call and that he delivered a plain brown envelope which was so ordinary that he couldn't remember it. Now, who was supposed to come at 7.30?'

'Bertram Heskith. I told you.'

'Exactly. So there were five minutes in which to escape. Five minutes for a determined man like Peter McGill to act quickly. Remember, his wife was generous, but she was not the sort of person to argue with him. And so, because of his decisive nature, Peter seized his opportunity.

'He had only five minutes, Charles, in which to escape from all those people whose cheerful faces we saw in the photograph. They all lived very close to him – they surrounded him, in fact – and it wasn't easy to leave unseen. He went out by the front door so that the watchful eyes would see him as usual and not be suspicious.

'There wasn't time to take anything with them. But, as Maureen ran through the garden to escape by the back way, she saw the sheets in the basket and couldn't stop herself taking them with her. She wasn't as hard as Peter. She wanted to take something from their past life, although the promise of a new life was so bright—'

Campion stopped suddenly. Chief Inspector Luke, who had begun to understand, was already moving towards the gate on his way to the nearest police telephone box.

♦

Mr Campion was at home in Bottle Street, Piccadilly, that evening when Luke called. The Chief Inspector came in cheerfully, and seemed very amused.

'It was the Irish Sweep,* not the football pools,[†] that they won,' he said. 'I got the details from the organizers. They've been considering what to do since they read the story in the newspapers. They're in touch with the McGills, of course, but Peter has taken great care to keep his good fortune secret. He must have known that his wife had a generous nature, and decided what he would do if he had a really big win. As soon as he got the letter which told him of his luck, he put his plan into action.'

Luke paused and shook his head in admiration. 'I can understand why he did it,' he said. 'Seventy-five thousand pounds is more than enough for two people, but not very much if it is shared around a very big family.'

'What will you do?'

'The police? Oh, officially, we are completely confused, and in the end we shall drop the matter. It's not our business — it's strictly a family affair.'

He sat down and took the drink that his host handed to him.

---

*Irish Sweep: a horse race in which large amounts of money can be won by betting.
[†]football pools: a system in which people try to win money each week by guessing the results of football games.

'Well, that's the end of the *Mary Celeste* house,' he said. 'I was completely fooled by it. I just didn't understand it. But good luck to the McGills! You know, Campion, you were right when you said that an unsolved mystery is only unsolved because no one wants to spoil it. How did you guess the solution?'

'The character of relatives who call at 7.30 in the morning makes me suspicious,' said Mr Campion.

The Invisible Man   G. K. *Chesterton*

In the cool blue of the late evening, at the corner of two steep streets in Camden Town in London, a young man of not less than twenty-four was looking into the window of a cake shop. He was a tall, strong, red-haired young man, with a determined face. His name was John Turnbull Angus. For him this shop held some kind of attraction, but this attraction was not completely explained by the cakes and sweets in the window.

He entered at last, and raised his hat to the young lady who was serving there. She was a dark, neat girl in black, with red cheeks and very quick, dark eyes. He walked through the shop into the back room, which was a sort of tearoom. After a short pause she followed him into the back room to write down his order.

His order was obviously a usual one. 'I want, please,' he said clearly, 'one halfpenny cake and a small cup of black coffee.' A moment before the girl turned away, he added, 'Also, I want you to marry me.'

The young lady of the shop stiffened suddenly, and said, 'Those are jokes I don't allow.'

The red-haired young man lifted his grey eyes and said, 'Really and truly, I am serious.'

The dark young lady had not taken her eyes off him and seemed to be studying him closely. Then, with a slight smile on her face, she sat down in a chair.

'Don't you think,' remarked Angus, 'that it's rather cruel to eat these halfpenny cakes? They might grow up into penny cakes. I shall give up these cruel sports when we are married, Laura.'

The dark young lady rose from her chair and walked to the window, clearly in a state of deep but not unsympathetic thought.

At last she swung round, returned to her chair, put her arms on the table and looked at the young man not unkindly, but with some annoyance.

'You don't give me time to think,' she said.

'I'm not such a fool,' he answered.

She was still looking at him; but she had grown more serious behind the smile.

'Before there is a minute more of this nonsense,' she said steadily, 'I must tell you something about myself.'

'I would like to hear it,' replied Angus.

'It's nothing that I'm ashamed of, and it isn't even anything that I'm specially sorry about. But what would you say if there were something which is not my fault but which troubles me like a bad dream?'

'In that case,' said the man seriously, 'I would suggest that you bring me another cake.'

'Well you must listen to the story first,' said Laura. 'To begin with, I must tell you that my father owned the inn called the Red Fish at Ludbury, and I used to serve people in the bar. Ludbury is a sleepy, grassy little place in eastern England. Half the people who came to the Red Fish were occasional business travellers. The rest were the most unpleasant people you can see, only you've never seen them. I mean little, lazy men who had just enough to live on, and nothing to do except lean about in the inn, in bad clothes that were just too good for them, and talk about horse racing. Even these characters were not very common at our inn; but there were two of them that were much *too* common. They both lived on money of their own, and were extremely lazy and dressed in very bad taste. But I was a bit sorry for them, because I half believe they came into our little empty bar because each of them was rather ugly; with the sort of ugly features which unsympathetic people laugh at. One of them was surprisingly small. He had a round black head and a neat black

84

beard, and bright eyes like a bird's; he wore a great gold watch chain, and he never came into the inn except dressed just too much like a gentleman to be one. He was not a fool, though he never did any work. He was strangely clever at all kinds of things that couldn't be the slightest use. He was always playing tricks with matches, or cutting toys out of fruit and making them dance. His name was Isidore Smythe; I can see him now, with his little dark face, amusing us in the inn.

'The other man was more silent and more ordinary, but for some reason he frightened me much more than poor little Smythe. He was very tall and thin, and light-haired. He might almost have been good-looking, but he had the most terrible squint I have ever seen or heard of. When he looked straight at you, you didn't know where you were yourself, and you certainly didn't know what he was looking at. I always thought this squint made the poor man rather bitter; while Smythe was ready to show off his tricks anywhere, James Welkin (that was the name of the man with the squint) never did anything except drink in the inn, and go for long walks by himself in the flat, grey country all round. All the same I think that Smythe, too, was a little self-conscious about being so small, though he hid it quite successfully. And so I was really confused, as well as surprised, and very sorry, when they both offered to marry me in the same week.

'Well, I did what I've since thought was perhaps a silly thing. But, after all, these men were my friends in a way; and I was frightened that they would think I refused them for the real reason, which was that they were so impossibly ugly. So I made up some nonsense of another sort, about never intending to marry anyone who had not made his own way in the world. I said that I could not live on family money like theirs which had not been earned. Two days after I had talked like this, the whole trouble began. The first thing I heard was that both of them had gone off to make their fortunes, as if they were in some silly children's story.

'Well, I've never seen either of them from that day to this. But I've had two letters from the little man called Smythe, and really they were rather exciting.'

'Ever heard of the other man?' asked Angus.

'No, he never wrote,' said the girl, after a moment's pause. 'Smythe's first letter was simply to say that he had started out to walk with Welkin to London; but Welkin was such a good walker that the little man dropped behind, and took a rest by the side of the road. He was picked up by some travelling show, and partly because he was so very small, and partly because he really was clever at his tricks, he got on well in show business. That was his first letter. His second was much more surprising, and I only got it last week.'

The man called Angus emptied his coffee cup and looked at her with patient eyes. Her own mouth twisted slightly with laughter as she went on: 'I suppose that you've seen the advertisements about this "Smythe's Silent Service"? Or you must be the only person who hasn't. Oh, I don't know much about it. It's some clockwork invention for doing all the housework by machinery. You know the sort of thing: "Press a button – A Servant Who Never Drinks." "Turn a handle – Ten Servants Who Never Eat." You must have seen the advertisements. Well, whatever these machines are, they are making a great deal of money; and they are making it all for that little man whom I knew down in Ludbury. I can't help feeling pleased that he is a success; but the plain fact is that I am frightened that he will arrive here at any minute and tell me that he has made his fortune – as he certainly has.'

'And the other man?' asked Angus quietly.

Laura Hope got to her feet suddenly. 'I haven't seen a line of the other man's writing and I haven't the slightest idea what or where he is. But it is of him that I am really frightened. He seems to be everywhere. It is he who has nearly driven me crazy. In fact, I think he has driven me crazy, because I've felt him where he couldn't have been, and I've heard his voice when he couldn't have spoken.'

'If he were the devil himself, he is defeated now that you have told somebody,' said Angus cheerfully. 'One goes out of one's mind all alone. When did you think you felt and heard our squinting friend?'

'I heard James Welkin laugh as plainly as I hear you speak,' said the girl, steadily. 'There was nobody there – I was standing just outside the shop at the corner, and could see down both streets at once. I had forgotten how he laughed, though his laugh was as strange as his squint. I had not thought of him for nearly a year. But a few seconds later the first letter came from the other man.'

'Did you ever make this invisible man speak or anything?' asked Angus, with some interest.

Laura trembled, and then went on in a steady voice: 'Yes. Just when I had finished reading the second letter from Isidore Smythe, announcing his success, I heard Welkin say: 'He won't have you, though.' It was quite clear, as if he were in the room. It is terrible; I think I must be crazy.'

'If you were really crazy,' said the young man, 'you would think that you were not. But certainly there seems to be something a little strange about this invisible gentleman. If you would allow me as a practical sort of man—'

As he spoke, there was a loud noise in the street outside, and a small motor car, driven at wild speed, pulled up at the door of the shop. In the same flash of time a small man in a tall, shiny hat stood stamping his feet in the outer room.

Angus, who up to now had pretended to be amused at the girl's story in order to hide the fact that he was troubled by it, showed his anxiety by marching immediately out of the inner room and meeting the stranger face to face. One look was quite enough for a man in love to recognize him. This very well-dressed little man with a pointed black beard, clever eyes, and neat but very nervous fingers, could only be the man just described to him: Isidore Smythe, who had made a fortune out of clockwork servants made of metal. For a moment the two men looked at each other with cold generosity, immediately understanding each other's air of possession.

Mr Smythe made no mention of it, but said simply and loudly: 'Has Miss Hope seen that thing on the window?'

'On the window?' repeated Angus in surprise.

'There's no time to explain other things,' said the rich man shortly. 'There's a matter here that we have to look into.'

He pointed his polished walking stick at the window. Angus was surprised to see that a long piece of paper had been stuck along the front of the glass. This had certainly not been on the window when he had looked into it some time before. He followed Smythe outside into the street, and looked at the paper. On it had been written in irregular letters: 'If you marry Smythe, he will die.'

'Laura,' said Angus, as he put his big red head into the shop, 'you're not crazy.'

'It's that man Welkin's writing,' said Smythe. 'I haven't seen him for years, but he's always annoying me. Five times in the last two weeks he's had threatening letters left at my flat, and I can't even find out who leaves them, and certainly not whether it's Welkin himself. The doorkeeper swears that no suspicious characters have been seen and now he's stuck this paper on a shop window, while the people in the shop—'

'Quite so,' said Angus, 'while the people in the shop were having tea. Well, sir, let me tell you I am pleased with your common sense in dealing so directly with the matter. We can talk about other things afterwards. The man cannot be very far off yet, since I swear there was no paper there when I last looked in the window, ten or fifteen minutes ago. But he's too far away to be followed, as we don't even know the direction. If you'll take my advice, Mr Smythe, you'll put this immediately in the hands of some detective, private rather than public. I know an extremely clever man, who has set up in business five minutes from here in your car. His name's Flambeau, and although his youth was a bit wild, he's a strictly honest man now, and his brains are worth money. He lives in Lucknow Flats, Hampstead.'

'That's strange,' said the little man. 'I live myself in Himalaya Flats, round the corner. Perhaps you would like to come with me. I can go to my rooms and sort out these strange Welkin documents, while you run round and get your friend the detective.'

'You're very good,' said Angus politely. 'Well, the sooner we act the better.'

Both men said goodbye to the girl with careful formality and jumped into the fast little car. As Smythe drove and they turned the corner of the street, Angus was amused to see a large advertisement for 'Smythe's Silent Service', with a picture of a headless machine carrying a cooking pan; under it were the words, 'A Cook Who Is Never Cross'.

'I use them in my own flat,' said the little black-bearded man with a laugh, 'partly for advertisement, and partly because they're convenient. Honestly, these big clockwork toys of mine do bring you coals or wine quicker than any live servants I've ever known, if you know which button to press. But I will also admit that such servants have their disadvantages, too.'

'Really?' said Angus. 'Is there something that they can't do?'

'Yes,' replied Smythe. 'They can't tell me who left those threatening letters at my flat.'

The man's motor car was small and quick like himself; in fact, like his silent servants, it was his own invention. Soon they turned a corner and were in the street which contained Himalaya Flats.

89

Opposite the flats was a bushy garden, and some way below that was a river. As the car swept into the street it passed, on one corner, a man selling hot soup. At the other end of the street, Angus could just see the blue figure of a policeman walking slowly. These were the only human shapes in that quiet scene.

The little car arrived at the right house like a bullet, and Smythe got out very quickly. He immediately asked the doorkeeper and a cleaner whether anybody or anything had passed them since he had last made inquiries. Then he and the slightly confused Angus went up in the lift to the top floor.

'Just come in for a minute,' said Smythe. 'I want to show you those Welkin letters. Then perhaps you will run round the corner and bring your friend.' He pressed a button hidden in the wall, and the door opened by itself.

It opened on a long, wide hall, of which the only unusual features were the rows of tall half-human machines that stood up on both sides. They were like the figures which dressmakers use. Like these figures, they had no heads, and like them, too, their chests and shoulders seemed to be slightly too large. Apart from this, they were not much more like a human figure than any machine at a railway station that is about human height. They had two great hooks like arms for carrying things, and they were painted bright green, or red, or black, so that the owner could tell one from the other. In every other way they were only machines and nobody would have looked twice at them. On this occasion, at least, nobody did. Because between the two rows of these machines lay something far more interesting. It was a white piece of paper written on in red ink. The little inventor seized it almost as soon as the door flew open. He handed it to Angus without a word. The red ink on it was actually not dry, and the message was: 'If you have been to see her today, I shall kill you.'

There was a short silence, and then Isidore Smythe said quietly: 'Would you like a drink? I rather feel as if I would.'

'No thank you. I would like to see Flambeau,' said Angus.

'Good,' said the other, clearly making an effort to be cheerful. 'Bring him round here as quickly as you can.'

But as Angus closed the front door behind him, he saw Smythe push back a button, and one of the clockwork figures moved smoothly from its place and slid along the floor carrying drinks. There did seem something rather strange about leaving the little man alone among those dead servants, who were coming to life as the door closed.

Six steps down from Smythe's flat, the cleaner was doing something with a bucket. Angus stopped and made him promise, by giving him money, to stay there until his return with the detective, and to watch carefully for any kind of stranger who came up those stairs. He hurried downstairs to the front hall and got the same promise from the doorkeeper. Angus learned from him that there was no back door. Not satisfied with this, he caught the policeman and persuaded him to stand opposite the entrance and watch it. Then, last of all, he paused for a moment to buy some chestnuts. He inquired how long the chestnut seller intended to stay in the neighbourhood.

The man turned up the collar of his coat and told him that he would probably be moving soon, as he thought that it was going to snow. It was true that the evening was growing grey and cold, but Angus managed to persuade him to remain where he was.

'Keep yourself warm with your own chestnuts,' he said seriously. 'Eat them all; I'll pay you well for them. I'll give you a pound if you'll wait here until I come back, and then tell me whether any man, woman, or child has gone into that house where the doorkeeper is standing.'

He then walked away quickly, with a last look at the house. 'I've made a ring round that room, now,' he said. 'They can't all four of them be friends of Welkin.'

Lucknow Flats were lower down the same hill on which

91

Himalaya Flats stood. Mr Flambeau's flat was on the ground floor. Flambeau, who was a friend of Angus's, received him in a little private room behind his office. It was decorated with swords and weapons of all kinds, strange objects from the East, bottles of Italian wine, ancient cooking pots and a grey cat. With him in the room was a small, dusty-looking priest who looked particularly out of place in these surroundings.

'This is my friend, Father Brown,' said Flambeau. 'I've often wanted you to meet him. Wonderful weather, this; a little cold for Southerners like me.'

'Yes, I think it will keep clear,' said Angus as he sat down.

'No,' said the priest quietly; 'it has begun to snow.'

And, as he spoke, the first snow began to fall gently across the darkening window.

'Well,' said Angus, seriously, 'I'm afraid I've come on business, and rather frightening business, too. The fact is, Flambeau, very close to your house is a man who badly wants your help. He is being threatened by an invisible enemy – a man whom nobody has ever seen.' Angus went on to tell the whole story of Smythe and Welkin. He began with Laura's story, and went on with his own; the strange laugh at the corner of two empty streets; the clear words spoken in an empty room. Flambeau grew more and more interested, and the little priest seemed to be forgotten, like a piece of furniture. When Angus came to the piece of paper stuck on the window, Flambeau rose and seemed to fill the room with his large shoulders.

'If you don't mind,' he said, 'I think that you'd better tell me the rest on the shortest road to this man's house. It seems to me that there is no time to lose.'

'With pleasure,' said Angus, and he also rose. 'Though he is safe enough for the present, since I've asked four men to watch the only door to his house.'

They went out into the street, the small priest following them like a small dog. He said, in a cheerful way, like one making conversation, 'How quickly the snow gets thick on the ground.'

As they walked along the streets, already powdered with silver, Angus finished his story; and by the time they reached the street where Smythe lived, he was able to turn his attention to the four guards whom he had left there. The chestnut seller, both before and after he had received a pound, swore that he had watched the door and seen no visitor enter. The policeman was even more sure. He said that he had had experience of criminals of all kinds, both well and badly dressed; he wasn't so foolish as to expect suspicious characters to look suspicious, so he had looked out for anybody, and there had been nobody. And when all three men stood round the doorkeeper, who was standing smiling in the doorway, the answer was even more certain.

'I've got a right to ask any man, rich or poor, what he wants in these flats,' said the big man, 'and I'll swear there's been nobody to ask since this gentleman went away.'

The unimportant Father Brown, who stood back, looking at the ground, said quietly: 'Has nobody been up and down stairs, then, since the snow began to fall? It began while we were all round at Flambeau's.'

'Nobody has been here, sir. You can believe me,' said the official with authority.

'Then what is that?' said the priest, and looked hard at the ground.

The others all looked down, too, and Flambeau swore in French. There was no doubt that down the middle of the entrance guarded by the doorkeeper, actually between his stretched legs, ran a pattern of grey footprints stamped on the white snow.

'Good heavens!' cried Angus; 'the Invisible Man!'

Without another word he turned and ran up the stairs with Flambeau following him; but Father Brown still stood and looked around him in the snow-covered street, as if he had lost interest in his own question.

Flambeau clearly wanted to break the door down with his big shoulder; but Angus, with more reason, if less imagination, felt about on the frame of the door until he found the invisible button. The door swung slowly open.

The hall had grown darker, although it was still lit here and there by the red light of the setting sun. One or two of the machines had been moved from their places for this or that purpose, and stood here and there around the half-dark room. But in the middle of them all, exactly where the paper with the red ink had lain, there lay something that looked very like red ink out of a bottle. But it was not red ink.

Flambeau simply said, 'Murder!' He ran into the flat and went into every corner and cupboard of it in five minutes. But if he expected to find a dead body, he found none. Isidore Smythe simply was not in the place, either dead or alive. After a careful search, the two men met each other in the outer hall. 'My friend,' said Flambeau, speaking French in his excitement, 'not only is the murderer invisible, but he also makes the murdered man invisible.'

Angus looked round the dark room full of clockwork figures and then trembled. One of the machines stood beside the blood, called perhaps by the dead man just before he fell. One of the hooks that the thing used for arms was slightly lifted, and Angus suddenly had the terrible thought that Smythe's own iron child had struck him down. The machines had attacked their master. But even if this were true, what had they done with him?

'Eaten him?' his imagination suggested. He felt sick for a moment at the idea of broken human remains swallowed and crushed by those headless clockwork figures.

With an effort he became calm, and said to Flambeau, 'The poor man has just disappeared completely. That simply can't happen in this world.'

'There is only one thing to be done,' said Flambeau. 'Whether the story belongs to this world or the other, I must go down and talk to my friend.'

He went down the stairs and passed the man with the bucket, who once again said that he had let no stranger pass. The doorkeeper and the chestnut seller also swore again that they had been watchful. But when Angus looked round for his fourth guard, he could not see him, and called out nervously: 'Where's the policeman?'

'I beg your pardon,' said Father Brown. 'That is my fault. I have just sent him down the road to find out something.'

'Well, we want him back soon,' said Angus, 'since the poor man upstairs has not only been murdered, but his body has disappeared.'

'How?' asked the priest.

'Father,' said Flambeau, after a pause, 'I believe it's more easily understood by a priest than a detective. No friend or enemy has entered the house, but Smythe is gone as if stolen by spirits. If that has a natural explanation, I—'

As he spoke he was interrupted by an unusual sight. The big, blue policeman ran round the corner. He came straight up to Brown.

'You're right, sir,' he said, 'they've just found poor Mr Smythe's body in the river.'

Angus put his hand to his head. 'Did he run down and drown himself?' he asked.

'He didn't come down, I'll swear,' said the policeman, 'and he wasn't drowned, since there's a knife wound over his heart.'

'Let us walk down the road a little,' said the priest to the others. Then, as they reached the corner, he remarked: 'How stupid of me! I forgot to ask the policeman if they found a large light brown bag.'

'Why light brown?' asked Angus in surprise.

'Because if it was any other colour, I must start again,' said Father Brown; 'but if it was light brown, the case is finished.'

'I am pleased to hear it,' said Angus. 'It hasn't begun, as far as I am concerned.'

'You must tell us all about it,' said Flambeau, with a strange simplicity, like a child.

Father Brown was silent for a moment. At last he said: 'Well, have you noticed this – that people never answer what you say? They answer what you mean – or what they think you mean. When those four quite honest men said that *no man* had gone into the building, they did not really mean that no man had gone into the building. They meant no man whom they could suspect of being the criminal. A man did go into the building, and did come out of it, but they never noticed him.'

'An invisible man?' inquired Angus with wide eyes.

'A man who was invisible to the mind,' said Father Brown.

A minute or two later he went on in a gentle voice, like a man who is thinking out what he has to say. 'Of course, you can't think of such a man, until you do think of him. That's the way in which he is so clever. But I came to think of him through two or three little things in the story that Mr Angus told us. First, there was the fact that Mr Welkin went for long walks. And then there were the two things the young lady said – things that couldn't be true. Don't get annoyed,' he added quickly when he noticed a sudden movement of Angus's head. 'She thought that they were true all right, but they couldn't be true. A person *can't* be quite alone in a street a second before she receives a letter. She can't be quite alone in a street when she starts to read a letter which she has just received. There must be somebody near her. He must be invisible to the mind.'

'Why must there be somebody near her?' asked Angus.

'Because,' said Father Brown, 'somebody must have brought her the letter.'

'Do you really mean to say,' asked Flambeau eagerly, 'that Welkin carried his competitor's letters to his lady?'

'Yes,' said the priest. 'Welkin carried the letters to his lady. You see, he had to.'

'Oh, this will drive me crazy,' exploded Flambeau. 'Who is this man? What does he look like? What is the usual dress of a man who is invisible to the mind?'

'He is dressed in a rather attractive red, blue and gold,' replied the priest immediately, 'and in these striking, and even showy clothes, he entered Himalaya Flats in front of eight human eyes; he killed Smythe, and came down into the street carrying the dead body in his arms—'

'Sir,' cried Angus, 'are you crazy, or am I?'

'You are not crazy,' said Father Brown, 'but you do not always notice things. You have not noticed such a man as this, for example.'

He stepped forward, and put his hand on the shoulder of an ordinary postman who was hurrying past them under the shade of the trees.

'Nobody ever notices postmen,' he said thoughtfully. 'But they have feelings like other men and they even carry large bags where a small body can be hidden quite easily.'

The postman, instead of turning naturally, had jumped with surprise and fallen against the garden fence. He was a thin fair-bearded man of very ordinary appearance, but as he turned a frightened face over his shoulder, he looked at all three men with a terrible squint.

Flambeau went back to his flat, since he had many things to attend to. John Turnbull Angus went back to the young lady at the shop, with whom he is now very comfortable. But Father Brown walked those snow-covered hills under the stars for many hours with a murderer, and what they said to each other will never be known.

The Case of the Thing That Whimpered
Dennis Wheatley

It would have been hard to find two men more different in appearance, character or lifestyle than the pair who were crossing the sunny garden of old Mark Hemmingway's home at Oyster Bay, Long Island.

Bruce was the old man's nephew. He was six feet two inches tall, with thick black hair and a strong good-looking face. He was a clever international lawyer. His companion, Neils Orsen, a delicate little man with large pale blue eyes like those of a Siamese cat, was a Swede. He had chosen to spend his life in the study of ghosts and spirits.

When their ship, the SS *Orion*, was three days out from England they had discovered that they had worked very close to one another in London. It was Orsen's first trip to the United States, and Bruce had invited him to spend at least a week at Oyster Bay to see what a real American home was like. They had come straight out to Long Island after the ship had arrived that morning.

Bruce pointed out a heavy, grey-haired figure relaxing in a chair outside the house. 'There's Uncle Mark, taking his usual Saturday afternoon rest.'

'Then please let us not wake him,' Orsen said.

'No, we won't do that; tea will be out in a minute, and he'll wake up then.'

They lowered themselves quietly into basket-chairs, and while Orsen leant back and closed his eyes, happy to enjoy the sweet smells of the garden, the big American bent down to pick up a newspaper from the grass. He loved facts and could never miss an opportunity to get information.

His eyes wandered over the page. There was more trouble in Europe, but that was nothing new. The daughter of the steel factory owner, Morgenfeld, had been kidnapped, and the reward which was being offered for the return of 6-year-old Angela had been increased to half a million dollars. She had been missing now for nearly two months. From her photographs she seemed to be a lovely child.

Suddenly Uncle Mark began to make strange noises in his sleep.

'Wake him,' said Orsen, opening his eyes. 'Wake him now.'

Bruce leant over and shook him slightly. 'Wake up, Uncle. Wake up!'

Mark Hemmingway gave a little cry, sat up and looked at them.

'Hello! So you've arrived. It's good to see you again, Bruce. And this is Mr Orsen whom you sent me the message about, eh?'

Orsen smiled, 'I am sorry if we woke you, sir, but you were having a bad dream, were you not?'

'Bad dream! Well, yes. How did you know?'

'That was not difficult – the noise that you were making. But I know quite a lot about dreams and I'll try to explain yours if you would like to tell me what it was about.'

'It's that storehouse. I can't get the place out of my thoughts.'

His nephew looked confused. 'Storehouse?'

'Yes, yes, storehouse. But never mind my troubles. Not when Mr Orsen has just arrived.'

'His real interest is ghost-hunting,' Bruce explained to his uncle with a smile, 'and though I don't think we'll find any ghosts round here, I hope that we'll be able to give him a good time.'

'We'll certainly do our best,' replied Mr Hemmingway. 'But as for ghosts, I just don't believe in such things, although I've had cause enough to believe in anything these last few weeks.'

'Thank you, Mr Hemmingway,' answered Orsen. 'It is most

kind of you to receive me in your lovely home. But what you say naturally excites my interest. I'm not surprised that you don't believe in ghosts, because they really appear very rarely. What people believe to be ghosts are nearly always the working of the imagination or tricks which have been played for a special purpose. Do tell me what it is that has recently caused you so much worry.'

'It's the terrible events that have happened one after the other in this storehouse that I was dreaming about just now.'

Bruce sat back and said, 'Let us have the details.'

His uncle paused for a moment and then, with a look at the stranger, he began: 'As Bruce may have told you, I'm a director of one of the biggest shops in New York. In recent months we have had to take a new storehouse in East 20th Street. It's not a good place because it's a long way from my shop and is built among blocks of poor flats down on the Lower East Side. But we needed it quickly and it was the best our agents could find. The building stands ten floors high, and the night watchman has two rooms on the top floor, an office and a sitting room. These are connected by a short walkway, one side of which is formed by the outer wall; the other is open except for a single handrail, so that the guard can look down over the whole storehouse. The two rooms and the walkway are built on a raised platform which can only be reached from the ground by some iron stairs. I'm giving you these details because the events in this place have provided a problem which the cleverest detectives in New York have failed to solve. But stop me if you're not interested.'

'No, no; please go on.'

'Right, then. The morning after we took the place, the night watchman was found on the ground floor very badly hurt. There had been no robbery; all the doors and windows were still locked. But somehow this unfortunate man had been attacked in the most violent manner while he was checking the storehouse, by someone or something that has the most unbelievable strength.'

'Something! Really, Uncle Mark! We don't have ghosts in New York,' Bruce interrupted, a half-smile twisting his mouth. 'What did the man say when he gained consciousness?'

'The poor man could tell us very little. The last thing he remembered was having just left the sitting room, at midnight, to check the building. He said that he paused for a moment outside because he thought he heard a strange whimpering sound like that of an animal in pain, and then suddenly the whole place seemed to melt – that's how he described it – and he found himself falling through the air to the stone floor below. He knew nothing more until he woke up in hospital.'

'Surely he can give some description of the thing that attacked him?' Bruce said.

'No. In the poor light he saw nothing. He had no time to look round. He says that his legs bent under him and he was thrown forward and down with great force.'

'That doesn't make sense.'

'It's the best description that he could give us and we were lucky to get that, as his terrible experience has had a serious effect on his mind.' Mark Hemmingway paused as two servants came out with the tea. When they had gone and he had poured out some tea for his guests, he went on: 'But that isn't all. We put a second night watchman in, and on the third night of his stay he was found just like the other one; but since he had a broken neck as well as other terrible injuries, he had no story to tell.'

'And the police, what did they say?' Orsen asked.

'They discovered nothing in their search, nothing at all. There was not a single sign of any living thing ever having entered the building after it had been closed for the night. But they did suggest one thing. It was this: that as this place had been empty for three years before we took it, a group of criminals might have been using it for unlawful purposes; and by these attacks on night watchmen they hoped to frighten the new owners away. That was the suggestion, but the police could not produce any proof that the storehouse had ever been used for anything, and although hundreds of people who live in that crowded neighbourhood were questioned, not one of them could remember ever having seen a vehicle of any kind drive up to the place by day or night until we arrived.'

'Why should they?' Bruce asked. 'People who live down on the Lower East Side don't generally regard the police as their friends. If criminals *are* working there, no one is going to risk being shot by them.'

'That's so. I think you're right about that. Anyway, after the death of the second watchman, it was very difficult to find another. But two days ago we employed a really strong man who knew nothing of the history of the place. This morning he was found alive, but terribly badly hurt. His face was beaten in, one arm was twisted behind his back and broken, and his chest was crushed. It was just as though some great force had picked him up and thrown him against the storehouse floor like a toy. In hospital, when he was conscious, he could hardly talk. All he could tell the police captain was: "Something whimpered at me – something whimpered, and then – and then I was thrown through the air." '

'So they both heard the strange whimpering,' Orsen said thoughtfully. 'What did the police chief have to say about that?'

'Nothing. He couldn't explain it at all. They are not even sure yet of the exact place where the attacks were made. The first man doesn't *remember* going down the iron stairs; but that doesn't mean much, as there were no signs of a struggle on the walkway, and all three bodies were found down below. One of the youngest of the policemen who are working on these crimes did suggest, although he felt a little silly about it, that there might be ghosts in the place and that this is the work of some sort of devil. Quite honestly, I have a strange feeling that the man might be right. No human has the strength to beat men as violently as that. Even if he had, they would remember something of what had happened to them.'

'I see,' said Neils Orsen. 'Of course there are rare cases when evil spirits take on violent and dangerous strength. But I'm more ready to believe the first suggestion, that your storehouse has been used for unlawful purposes, and that somebody is particularly anxious to frighten you into giving it up . . . Still, I would very much like to try to solve the mystery. May I take on the duties of night watchman tonight?'

'Good heavens, no! You're my guest. I cannot allow — well, anyone like yourself to spend a night in that place alone.'

Orsen smiled. 'I see you're thinking of my size. But I would carry a gun. We could also have a police guard outside the building, and if they are criminals who are doing this, my shots would bring immediate help. But if it really is a ghost or an evil spirit, I am far better able to deal with it than the most experienced policeman in New York.'

'No, no. You've never met the sort of criminals we have in this country. They are killers and they would murder you before the police even got through the door. I'll tell you what I will do though, since you're so interested. I'll take you and Bruce to have a look round the place tomorrow afternoon.'

The three of them, with a police officer, made a careful search of the storehouse, but they found nothing new. The policeman was sure that the attacks had been made on the floor of the storehouse, but Orsen thought that they had happened while the watchman was up on the walkway, because the only man who could give even a partly sensible account of what had happened could not remember coming down the iron stairs.

For this reason it was up on the walkway that he put the scientific instruments that he had brought with him. These were two cameras with flashlights, which would take pictures if anyone crossed the walkway, and a sound-recording machine of his own invention which was so sensitive, he said, that it could pick up voices from the world of spirits.

The police officer watched his preparations with amusement, while Hemmingway and Bruce only hid their disbelief out of politeness. But Orsen stated, with great confidence, that he intended to find out whether the attacker was a ghost or a man.

On the following morning they visited the storehouse again. The locks on the doors and windows had not been touched – but Orsen's two cameras and his recording machine were no longer up on the walkway. They lay in small pieces on the floor below.

The little Swede began to collect the bits, and with Bruce's help, put them all in a bag. But although the cameras could not help them, they found, when they returned to Oyster Bay, that the material on the recording machine could be played. Orsen tried it on another machine.

For a moment a low, whimpering cry filled the pleasantly sunny room with the cold breath of evil. Then the sound suddenly stopped.

'Well, the watchman certainly didn't imagine that!' said Bruce with a nervous laugh.

'No,' Orsen's large, pale blue eyes filled with a sudden light; 'and that's not the sort of noise a killer makes when he is about to murder someone. I really believe now that we're on the track of an *Ab-human*.'

'What is that?' asked Bruce.

'It's not a ghost in the ordinary sense at all. By that I mean it's not the spirit of a dead person forced to remain on earth, but a bodiless force – something that has somehow made its way up out of the Great Depths and found a gateway by which it can get back into this world. Such appearances are very rare, but to a scientist like myself extremely interesting. Now nothing can

104

prevent me from going back to the storehouse this evening and spending the night there.'

'I won't allow you to do that alone,' Bruce said quickly.

'I shall be pleased to have your company,' Orsen smiled.

Orsen made many careful preparations for the night's watch, because he knew that he and Bruce might have to face great danger. Both men carried guns in case the ghost was found to be a murderous human after all. Both also had magic items which had proved to be powerful against evil spirits. Bruce felt like laughing at these protective measures, but the little man was so serious about them that Bruce had no difficulty in hiding his amusement.

At nine o'clock they went to the storehouse. The place was badly lit and every packing case seemed to throw the shadow of some terrible being after them as they walked.

'Brrr – I wouldn't like to be the man whose job it is to stay here all night, whether there are ghosts or not,' said Bruce.

'It'll be more cheerful upstairs in the watchman's sitting room,' Orsen said quietly. When they had climbed the iron stairs, he began to explain his plans to Bruce.

'I intend to go round the whole place every hour, but I want you to remain in this room, Bruce. You are not to leave it whatever happens. You will stay by the door and watch the walkway outside with your gun ready and protect my back each time I go downstairs. Even if all you see is a shadow, shoot immediately. Light will always drive back the Powers of Darkness, at least for a moment. The flash from your gun will give me just enough time to say the words which will protect us from evil spirits.'

At ten o'clock Orsen went round the storehouse for the first time. Bruce stood in the doorway of the sitting room and guarded the walkway with his gun, until his little friend was hidden from sight in the shadows. He then returned to his seat in the room. A quarter of an hour later, Orsen quietly appeared again. Bruce jumped nervously to his feet and asked: 'Well?'

'No, nothing,' replied Orsen.

Conversation was difficult. The frightening silence all round them seemed to forbid even a whisper. The sun had shone on the roof all day and the heat in the room was uncomfortable. Both men had taken their coats off.

The minutes dragged on. Eleven o'clock came at last, and once again the little Swede went out into the unfriendly shadows beyond the warm sitting room, while Bruce watched from the door. Once again he returned with nothing to report.

Time seemed to stand still. Bruce suddenly began to think of the people in the town outside who were laughing and talking without a worry in the world. They would sleep in warm, comfortable beds tonight, while he sat waiting for some terrible, unknown thing to come out of the half-darkness, violently attack him and then throw him away like a broken toy.

He shook himself. He was not easily frightened, and if his gun and strength could have been of any use, there would have been no fear in his heart. But the calm, clever little man opposite him really believed in ghosts and spirits, and had told him of their terrible power to harm human beings.

The minutes went slowly by. Suddenly Orsen began to move uncomfortably in his seat, his long, thin fingers tapping on his knees. Bruce watched him with quick anxiety. Then a low whimpering cry broke the stillness of the quiet room.

Immediately Orsen jumped to his feet and ran to the door. As he ran, he called out some Latin words from an ancient prayer for protection against evil spirits. Bruce quickly took hold of his gun and followed. When Orsen stepped out onto the walkway, the whole thing moved beneath him. He almost lost his balance. His legs were unable to support him, and he was thrown violently forward into space.

At the same moment Bruce, who was still at the door of the sitting room, had seen that both the walkway and the wall behind it were turning by ninety degrees. In another moment, the block of wall would fall forwards into the place where the walkway floor had been. In the dark space behind the falling wall Bruce saw a shadowy shape. His gun fired and fired with a bright red flame until it was empty. There was a cry of pain and the wall began to move back up again, bringing the floor of the walkway up with it.

'Neils! Neils!' Bruce cried as he looked out into the half-darkness. To his great relief he heard an answering cry. Orsen had managed to hold onto the single rail of the walkway as he was thrown outwards. It was a frightening moment as he hung there by one hand, eighty feet above the stone floor below. But as the wall moved back into place, the floor of the walkway rose with it and brought him back to safety. Bruce, whose face was white with fear, pulled him into the sitting room, and for a few moments they both stood there breathing heavily.

When their strength had returned, they set to work to solve the mystery of the hidden entrance. With the help of an iron bar they managed to pull down the block of wall, and they saw how the floor of the walkway turned over as they did so.

'That's what happened to the unfortunate night watchmen!' Orsen said. 'An eighty-foot drop! That's why they remembered nothing and were so badly injured.'

'Come on! Let's see what's in here,' Bruce whispered and pointed to the dark space which the opening of the wall had left. As he stepped forward, his foot touched something. He pointed the beam of his flashlight at the ground and bent down. He saw that it was the body of a man. Together they dragged it into the light. It was not a pretty sight. The man had clearly not been very fond of soap and water. He was bleeding badly from several bullet wounds and was quite dead.

'I suppose I must have killed him,' said Bruce slowly. 'What do you think he was doing?'

'Who can say? Clearly he has been coming and going to this secret room for some time and entering it by a hidden door. Then when your uncle's people moved in, he thought he would frighten them away by killing off your night watchmen. He just had to wait for the men to begin their midnight check and then pull a handle. Too simple!'

Suddenly the whimpering started again. Bruce felt the hair on the back of his neck stand up, but Orsen calmly turned on his flashlight and shone it round the secret room. Its beam fell on a child.

'Angela Morgenfeld!' cried Bruce in surprise. With two steps he reached her, and picked the thin, frightened little thing up in his arms. 'Orsen,' he cried, 'do you realize that this is the factory owner's daughter, who was kidnapped over two months ago?'

He laughed then with a mixture of relief and excitement. 'That man that I killed must have been coming in every night over the roof to feed her. And this poor child is your great *Ab-human*.'

Orsen smiled. 'I would rather have found her, though, than the most interesting spirit from another world. But wait until we are back in England next month and I'll certainly show you a real ghost.'

Bruce laughed. 'I'll be with you.'

ACTIVITIES

The Blue Cross

Before you read

1 Look up these words in your dictionary.

   *arrest   heath   inch   inspector   invisible   relief   shilling
   suspect*

   Match the words with the phrases:

   a Feel that something is probably true
   b A feeling people have when a bad experience has ended
   c What policemen do to criminals
   d Something that you can't see
   e A title for a police officer
   f Equal to 2.54 centimetres
   g An old British coin
   h An area of open land with few trees or bushes

After you read

2 Describe the part these play in the story:
   a Valentin   **b** Flambeau   **c** Father Brown   **d** the blue cross.
3 Discuss how and why Father Brown protects himself against
   Flambeau.

Philomel Cottage

Before you read

4 Imagine you are twenty years old and single, and you are suddenly
   left a lot of money by a relative. Do you think this would affect your
   relationship with people? If so, how?

5 Find these words in your dictionary. They are all in the story.

butcher   cottage   inn   nightingale   skeleton

Match each new word with a group of connected words.

a song, nest, wings

b traveller, bar, hotel

c bones, dead, human body

d meat, knife, chicken

e house, country, small

After you read

6 Answer the questions.

a What first makes Alix suspicious of her husband?

b What does she discover about his past?

c How does she save herself?

7 Work in pairs. Take the parts of Alix and Dick, and continue the story.

Student A: You are Alix. Explain to Dick why you phoned him and what happened before he arrived.

Student B: You are Dick. Ask questions, explain why you came to Philomel Cottage, and try to calm Alix.

An Unpleasant Man

Before you read

8 Do you know the American English words for these British words? Can you add other pairs of words to your list?

trousers   an underground train   petrol   a tap
a handbag   a flat

9 Check the meanings of these words in your dictionary.

agency/agent   *sergeant*   *staff officer*   *trunk call*

a In what type of organizations would you find a *sergeant*?

b What does a *staff officer* do?

c What is a more modern phrase for a *trunk call*?

d What kinds of businesses use the term *agency*?

e What kind of job does a secret *agent* have?

After you read

10 Who:

a died during a bank robbery?

b was put to death for murder?

c was a witness against him?

d came to England because of his job?

e wants to disappear?

f dies in Hawthorn House?

11 Discuss differences in the words used by speakers of your language. Can you tell which country, area or town they come from?

The Unlucky Theatre

Before you read

12 Do you believe in ghosts? Have you ever seen or heard one? What are the ghosts in stories usually like?

After you read

13 What real event does Lindsey believe has brought bad luck to the theatre?

14 You are Fernaghan. Describe what you saw, heard and felt on the night you spent in the theatre.

The Mezzotint

Before you read

15 Find the word *mezzotint* in your dictionary.

Tick (✓) the three options that have a connection with *mezzotints*.

_____ **a** a picture

_____ **b** on plastic

_____ **c** noise and colour

_____ **d** a piece of music

_____ **e** light and shadow

_____ **f** on metal

After you read

16 Describe how the picture changes through the story.

17 Tell the story that lies behind the picture.

Family Affair

Before you read

18 What was the mystery of the *Mary Celeste*? What other mysterious and unexplained events from the past do you know about?

19 Check the meanings of these words in your dictionary:

chestnut   penny

Which word refers to:

a something that grows on a tree

b something that you can spend

After you read

20 Why are these important to the solving of the case?

a a pair of sheets   **b** savings books   **c** a ladder

d a brown envelope

21 Discuss what happened to the McGills on the day they disappeared, and what they are doing now. Would you behave in the same way?

22 Campion says: 'The character of relatives who call at 7.30 in the morning makes me suspicious.' Do you agree with him?

The Invisible Man

Before you read

23 What do you think would happen if you walked into a café, sat down, ordered a cup of coffee and a cake and asked the waitress or waiter to marry you?

24 Check the meanings of these words in your dictionary:

clockwork   squint

Choose (i) or (ii) to complete each sentence.

a If a factory runs like *clockwork*, it is:

(i) inefficient   (ii) efficient.

b A *clockwork* toy:

(i) can move   (ii) can't move.

c A person with a *squint* has a problem with his or her:

(i) ears   (ii) eyes.

d If you take a *squint* at something, you:

(i) have a look at it   (ii) throw something at it.

After you read

25 Explain these remarks.

a 'Those are jokes I don't allow.'

b 'The first thing I heard was that both of them had gone off to make their fortunes . . .'

c 'If you were really crazy, you would think that you were not.'

d 'But I will also admit that such servants have their disadvantages, too.'

e 'My friend, not only is the murderer invisible, but he also makes the murdered man invisible.'

f 'He is dressed in a rather attractive red, blue and gold . . .'

26 Work in pairs, and act out this conversation.

Student A: You are John Angus. Tell Laura how the 'Invisible Man' was caught.

Student B: You are Laura. Ask questions, and express your own feelings now.

The Case of the Thing That Whimpered

Before you read

27 Check the meanings of the words in *italics* in your dictionary. Answer these questions.

a What kinds of creature can *whimper*?

b Can you think of a situation when a child would *whimper*?

c Why do criminals *kidnap* people?

d Do you know about any famous *kidnapping* cases?

e Where would you see a *handrail*?

f Why are *handrails* useful?

After you read

28 Fill the gaps to complete the story.

Two months earlier, a 6-year-old girl, Angela Morgenfeld, was ¹............... . Since then, she has been held in a ²............... . Two ³............... have been seriously injured and one has been killed. The office, sitting room and walkway are on a raised ⁴..............., but the men are all found on the ⁵............... eighty feet below. When the kidnapper pulls a ⁶..............., part of the wall opens and the ⁷............... turns over. The ⁸............... sound is made by the kidnapped child.

29 Discuss why Orsen feels that the presence of ghosts may explain the mystery. How does he discover that no ghost is involved?

Writing

30 Which story did you enjoy most? Why?

31 Compare the appearance, character and methods of two of the 'detectives'.

32 Explain the part played in the collection by one of these:

   a ghosts **b** money **c** love **d** hate

33 Write a newspaper report of one of these events:

   a the arrest of Flambeau. **b** the death of Gerald Martin.

34 Write a letter:

   a from Mrs McGill to her sister a year after her disappearance.

   b from Joe Spencer to a friend of his brother's after Harris's arrest.

35 Choose one of the stories and explain the changes that would be needed if it were set in your country.

Answers for the activities in this book are available from your local
Pearson Education office or contact: Penguin Readers Marketing Department,
Pearson Education, Edinburgh Gate, Harlow, Essex, CM20 2JE.